Transforming Trauma

A holistic approach to trauma recovery and how psilocybin mushrooms helped me to escape the darkness of PTSD

Darcy Dudeck

Platypus Publishing

Copyright © 2023 by Darcy Dudeck

All rights reserved.

No portion of this book may be reproduced in any form without written permission from the publisher or author, except as permitted by Canadian and U.S. copyright law.

The information presented is the author's opinion and does not constitute any health or medical advice. The publisher and the author make no guarantees concerning the level of success you may experience by following the advice and strategies contained in this book, and you accept the risk that results will differ for each individual.

To the best of my ability, I have re-created events, locales, people, and organizations from my memories of them. In order to maintain the anonymity of others, in all instances I have changed the names and identifying details *of individuals and places, and the details of events. I have also changed some identifying characteristics, such as physical descriptions, occupations, and places of residence.*

Book Cover by Darcy Dudeck
First edition 2023

For everyone who has gone through it or is going through it.
You are never alone.

Contents

Prologue		1
1.	At My Lowest Point	2
2.	Medication Does Not Work For Everyone	7
3.	Post Traumatic Recovery	11
4.	The Subpoena	15
5.	Am I Dreaming?	24
6.	The Diagnosis	29
7.	Downward Spiral	33
8.	Flashbacks	44
9.	The Realities of Working in a Prison	52
10.	You Can't Reason With a Psychopath	61
11.	Eye Movement Desensitization & Reprocessing (EMDR)	66
12.	Realistic Recovery	74
13.	The Nervous System's Role in Trauma	79
14.	My Recovery Plan	86

15.	Relaxing the Nervous System	91
16.	Journaling, Mindfulness and Connection	98
17.	Making the Decision to Try Microdosing Psilocybin	103
18.	The Protocols	106
19.	Preparing to Microdose	113
20.	My Experience Microdosing Psilocybin	115
21.	Final Thoughts on Microdosing	122
22.	Conclusion	125
	About the Author	127

Prologue

Thirteen months after he violently reoffended came the day that changed my life forever. That day, I felt like my world started spinning out of control and I had no idea how to stop it. That was the beginning of a journey that would change my life completely.

Chapter 1

At My Lowest Point

There are parts of ourselves that we keep deeply hidden away from everyone. Sometimes even from ourselves if we are in denial about what, and how serious our injuries are. At least this was the case for me.

I kept most of what I was struggling with to myself, which also meant I was isolating myself from everyone I cared about. I did this because I didn't think my friends and family would be able to understand. I also felt a lot of shame for struggling so much at times. How do you tell your friends and family that it feels impossible to go on? That you're not even sure you want to go on. That you feel like you're a complete failure. It just seemed easier to keep everything to myself.

At my lowest points I was dealing with sleep deprivation, nightmares, extreme hypervigilance, flashbacks, panic attacks and soul crushing anxiety. It was a terribly lonely and sad time in my life. I carried a lot. It was heavy and I carried it alone. I was alone most of the time with my destructive thoughts. I went to sleep sad and woke up to nightmares and panic attacks. Sadness, fear, anxiety and shame were always with me. Every day felt like a never ending battle just to survive.

It felt as though I had fallen into a deep dark hole with no way out. If you've ever fallen down that hole you'll understand what I'm talking about. There are demons down there and their only purpose is to keep you down there. They constantly judge you, mock you and tell you that no one cares about you.

They have this way of getting you to believe that you are worthless and that no one could ever love you the way you are. They tell you you're a broken mess, that you're not good enough, that you'll never get better so you should just stop trying. A lot of people can't understand thoughts like this and that's why I kept myself so isolated. I was afraid if anyone knew, they would judge me, and at the time I was already judging myself incredibly harshly. I just couldn't face judgement from anyone else.

The exhaustion I felt also kept me in isolation. It's very difficult to explain this type of exhaustion. It doesn't come from just a lack of sleep. This kind of exhaustion comes from being in a constant state of fight/flight/freeze. My nervous system was always on high alert, looking for signs of danger everywhere I went. No matter the environment I was in, I was constantly scanning my surroundings looking for potential danger. I still do this. This is not something that can be easily controlled and if there is a way to control it, I haven't figured it out yet.

I used to feel emotionally numb all the time. It felt like nothing could shock me anymore. I didn't feel joy or happiness and could barely even remember what those felt like. I think we numb ourselves in order to keep going on and so we can keep doing our jobs. But when we numb ourselves to stop feeling the bad stuff we are also no longer able to feel the good stuff in life either.

I felt so alone all of the time, even when I was with people. Being with people when you have to keep a mask on is a very lonely feeling. Just keep smiling and laughing so no one sees how broken you actually feel.

I didn't feel safe anywhere, including my own home at times. I began double locking my doors and sleeping with weapons beside my bed. I still sleep with a weapon next to my bed, but the difference now is I don't check to make sure it's there every time I wake up throughout the night.

Throughout this journey, I've had people in my life who meant well tell me that I needed to go back to work. They said it would help me feel better. But how could that help me feel better when being at work is what caused my injury in the first place? The thought of being at work, in any workplace at the time was extremely anxiety inducing. They told me it wasn't healthy for me to be living like a retired person at my age. What they failed to recognize, or even try to understand, was that I was fighting to regain control over my life, not living like I was retired. The fact that people couldn't understand this was frustrating and kept me isolating myself.

I'm sharing all of this with you so you can see just how bad things had become for me at one time. Not to gain sympathy, but so you know there is hope. I've come a long way since then and I barely recognize the person I used to be. It wasn't easy though. Essentially, I had to burn my old life down to the ground before I could start to rebuild something better. It was a grueling process but I have walked out of the ashes a much better version of myself. That's the beauty of this journey. I get to recreate myself and the life I truly want to live. And you can do the same.

***

Since that day my life was forever changed, I have learned a great deal about complex trauma and post traumatic injuries. I've also implemented many different things into my post traumatic recovery plan, including the use of psychedelic medicine.

Have you ever wondered what psychedelics can do for PTSD? Have you ever thought about using psychedelics to help in your post traumatic recovery? I also wondered before I started microdosing psilocybin mushrooms, more commonly known as magic mushrooms. It's unconventional, but it has taken my recovery to the next level and I would not be where I am today without it.

Many people who receive a PTSD diagnosis are not presented with a lot of options. Basically, a doctor tells you what medication they think is appropriate for you. Then you are referred to a psychologist or a psychiatrist, or in some cases, both. The emphasis is placed on medication and therapy but no one really tells you what you can expect in therapy.

No one tells you that the traumas that caused your injury are not all in your mind. They don't tell you that trauma is also trapped in your nervous system. Nobody tells you about alternative therapies or how to start healing your nervous system. No one tells you that you cannot recover while working in the same environment where your injury happened. And I learned the hard way that you absolutely cannot recover while working in the same environment that caused your injury. I was not the exception to this and neither are you.

I am not a trained expert on complex trauma recovery. I am simply someone who has walked the path. Someone who continues to walk the path. Someone who has utilized therapy, as well as a few other healing modalities to recover from complex trauma.

If you have ever considered using psychedelics in your post traumatic recovery, follow me as I take you through the realities of what it's like to live with a post traumatic stress injury, and what it's like to recover using both conventional and unconventional methods.

Chapter 2

Medication Does Not Work For Everyone

It's important for you to know that I am not anti medication. I believe that medication has benefits and is helpful for some people. However, I did not feel like it was the right option for me. PTSD had me feeling numb for so long and I know that these medications can have a numbing effect on emotions. I was not interested in prolonging the numbing, so I chose not to use it.

PTSD also affects your nervous system as well as your entire body. Not just your mind. So while the medication may help numb your mind or help you sleep, it does very little to treat the effects trauma has on your nervous system. And if you're not doing anything to treat your nervous system, then you are only doing half of the work and this can make recovery feel almost impossible.

Medication can help relieve some of the symptoms a person experiences when they have PTSD but it does not cure it. And for approximately 20 - 30 percent of people with PTSD, medication does not work. Have you heard the term "treatment resistant PTSD"? When they say treatment resistant, they're referring to the use of medication and therapy, specifically Cognitive Behavioural Therapy (CBT). It's treatment resistant because PTSD affects much more than your mind. And changing your thoughts does very little to relax your nervous system. So in my opinion, when someone is deemed as treatment resistant, perhaps it's because the right treatments for that person have not been explored.

Two years into post traumatic recovery, my family doctor retired, and I started seeing a new doctor who insisted that I need to be on antidepressant medication. This doctor did not listen to a word I said, or to any of the concerns I had about taking this medication. She also did not listen when I told her I had been in trauma recovery for two years, unmedicated, and making progress. I tried to explain that at this point I felt like starting medication would be like taking steps backwards. I had already made too much progress without medication and telling her this fell on deaf ears.

It was frustrating to say the least. This doctor, who knew absolutely nothing about me, was telling me what she thought was best for me without listening to anything I was saying, or addressing any of my concerns regarding the medication she was trying to push on me. My psychologist had sent a report to her but she told me she did not have time to read it. I wondered how she could have an opinion about my recovery plan when she couldn't even take the time to read a report detailing everything I'd been experiencing. I left that appointment and had a panic attack in my car.

I was upset for many reasons that day. I felt unheard. I felt like any input I had about my own recovery plan was not valid. I felt like this doctor, who barely knew me, was making decisions about my recovery without taking the time to learn any information about me. And by pushing pills on me that I told her I did not want to take. I felt completely invalidated.

That was the day I made the decision to keep the medical doctors out of my trauma recovery. It was also the day I made the decision to look for a new family doctor.

I had heard about people using psychedelic medicine to treat PTSD and I'll admit, I was intrigued. After that dreadful appointment with Dr. Pill Pusher, I decided to start doing some research on the topic. I was mostly interested in using psilocybin and microdosing it.

I grew up during a time where we were taught to view psilocybin mushrooms and other psychedelics through the lens of fear. They were considered dangerous drugs and we were taught to fear drugs. I've learned that these mushrooms, as well as other psychedelics, are nothing to fear. They are not the dangerous drugs we were taught to believe. They are an incredible medicine and they are something that has helped me to get to a place in recovery I was afraid I would never reach.

I did not jump into using psychedelics quickly though. I spent a couple of months doing some research before I finally made the decision to give it a try. I talked to my psychologist about it as well. It is illegal to possess psilocybin mushrooms and the use of psychedelics for treating PTSD is not a conventional therapy, so he knew very little about it. But he didn't discourage me. That's the sign of a good psychologist. Someone who doesn't tell you what they think is best for you. Someone who listens without judgment. Someone that encourages you and lets you have some input into your own recovery plan.

Chapter 3

Post Traumatic Recovery

As I mentioned, I am no expert on the topic of trauma recovery. I am just someone, like you, that's experienced many traumatic events that led to being diagnosed with a post traumatic stress injury.

My PTSD is related to my career in Criminal Justice. I began my career in Corrections 22 years ago. For the first 12 years I worked in a maximum security prison. I left that position after realizing how detrimental it was to my well being. From there I worked in an office where I processed arrest warrants for offenders who breached their community sentences. I enjoyed this work, however, it was a temporary position and I had other goals. After leaving this position, I became a Community Corrections Worker (CCW). I worked in this capacity for a little over 2 years before beginning my new role as a Probation Officer. These positions all contributed to the decline of my mental health, however, the position of Community Corrections Worker left the most scars.

I am sharing my journey with you now because I wish I would have known some of the stuff I've learned about trauma recovery since being diagnosed, at the beginning of my own journey. I fumbled through the process, educating myself on everything trauma related and now I'm sharing it with you so you know you're not alone and to hopefully make your journey a bit easier to navigate. One thing I can promise you is there is life after trauma, even though it might not feel like it right now.

From the beginning of this journey I made it my mission to learn as much as possible about my injury and how to recover. I have read a few books on this subject written by experts, however so much of what I read was just so technical and offered very little on the reality of the recovery journey. While I appreciate and value the experts' opinions and advice, I always felt less alone when talking with others who have gone through similar situations.

Experts definitely have their place in trauma recovery. However, if you haven't experienced this type of injury, then you really don't understand everything those of us on this journey go through on a daily basis. The experts are tremendously important in our recovery, but so is making connections with others who understand. Connecting with others who have walked similar paths can be extremely therapeutic and I encourage you to do so.

My trauma recovery journey has been extremely difficult at times. In fact there are moments where I didn't want to live anymore. Having gone through this process, I feel like I have come out as a better version of myself. Not only has this been a journey of recovery and self discovery, but it has also been a spiritual journey. I feel like I am becoming a better version of myself everyday. I have gained a lot of self awareness, I am more confident in my ability to set clear boundaries and I am mentally stronger than ever. I hope that my words will help and inspire you along your own recovery journey.

I've learned that post traumatic recovery looks a bit different for everyone. It's about trying new things to find out what works for you and what doesn't. And then implement the things that work for you into designing your own recovery plan. My own trauma recovery plan includes several things in addition to therapy. Yoga, meditation, writing, walking in nature, photography and microdosing psilocybin are a few things that have helped me along this journey and continue to do so.

The recovery process is not about reaching an end goal. Sure, we all want to think that once we go through therapy we'll be cured, but that is not how recovery works. Post traumatic recovery is about more than just healing past traumas. Recovery is a lifestyle and it's about learning a new and healthier way to live. It's about learning to make space for your traumas because they won't disappear. It's a journey of self discovery. It's about learning to recognize triggers so they become easier to manage and lead to less panic attacks and a better quality of life. It's about learning what to do to relax your nervous system because it plays a huge role in trauma recovery.

There are no shortcuts or easy ways through the process of post traumatic recovery. It's hard and exhausting work. But I promise you, it's worth it. There are days that you will be feeling much better and think it's all uphill from here. But then you end up backsliding, and that's okay. It doesn't mean you're failing. Ups and downs are all part of the process.

Post traumatic recovery teaches you how to be patient with yourself. How to treat yourself with the same compassion you can easily offer others who are struggling. It teaches you how to forgive yourself and accept yourself for who you are. Post traumatic recovery is so much more than just healing past traumas. It can be a wonderful, life changing journey of self discovery if you let it be.

Chapter 4

The Subpoena

Thirteen months after he violently reoffended came the day that changed my life forever.

It was like any other day working as a Community Corrections Worker (CCW). I was at home, sitting at the kitchen table, finishing up some reports I had been writing when my phone rang. It was someone from the office calling to let me know that a subpoena had arrived for me.

I immediately froze. Having to testify in court is not something I enjoy and the thought of it gave me severe anxiety. My heart was racing when I asked which client the subpoena was for. I had a feeling the answer was going to be that it was for Dave, and I was right. The person on the other end of the phone confirmed my worst fear and we concluded our conversation.

I hung up from that call, put my head down on the table and started crying. That was the exact moment I knew I was broken.

That's also when the nightmares began happening on a regular basis, along with waking up regularly to panic attacks.

I sat at the kitchen table for a long time. I felt like I couldn't move. My mind drifted back to that month in 2017, where a series of events would lead to the court serving me with a subpoena today.

***

Dave had been one of the worst offenders I've ever had to work with. In fact, he was undoubtedly the worst of them all. I know my PTSD took years to develop, however, Dave was what finally broke me.

When I first started working with high risk sex offenders Cathy was my partner and then eventually Jill was my partner. Both of these women were exceptional and amazing to work with. I couldn't have asked for better partners to work with during all of the disturbing adventures we had as CCWs.

Dave is a very dark and extremely dangerous offender. Getting to know him was a terrifying adventure. In the beginning he openly hated us. He hated all of probation and the justice system in general, and he made sure to let us know every chance he got. He was very difficult to deal with and did not like answering our questions. He had a court ordered curfew and hated being curfew checked. He always made it as difficult as he possibly could.

He once told us he knew our curfew checking pattern because he kept track of each and every curfew check on a calendar. That's when we decided we needed to switch things up a bit. What good is a curfew check if the guy knows when it's happening? Cathy and I curfew checked him twice per week but we also asked another pair of CCWs to check him on nights they were out. This sent Dave into an absolute rage.

We met with him at a local coffee shop one evening where he confronted us with that rage. He asked what the fuck we thought we were doing having him curfew checked so much. We tried to explain that these checks were not limited to twice per week. He was so enraged and wasn't listening to us. He sat there staring at us with his cold dead eyes. He didn't even blink, which was unsettling, and then suddenly his eyes started to twitch. I had never witnessed anything like it before.

Abruptly, he stood up from the table and pointed his finger in Cathy's face. His anger exploded and he started yelling. He was directing all of his anger onto Cathy. He was screaming all sorts of insults at her and said he hated her and had always hated her. I quickly stood up and told him the meeting was over and then he turned his anger towards me. After he called me names, he told me to fuck off before storming out of the coffee shop. Cathy and I just sat there for a minute before leaving, wondering if what had just happened was real.

We sat in the car and pretty much couldn't even debrief at that moment. We were stunned because what we had just witnessed was terrifying. We thought that must be what Dave's victims saw right before he attacked. We had just sent a very angry rapist out into the world. We finally managed a quick debrief of the situation before finishing up our shift, going our separate ways and pretending life was normal. From there I went to the park to meet a friend for a walk.

Dave is a violent rapist, a stalker and a self professed "collector". Once he became caught up in his offence cycle is when things felt like they shifted in a dark and frightening way. And it all felt like it began on the night he lost control in that coffee shop.

My friend and I had just finished our walk when my work phone rang. It was Dave calling and I was not at all prepared for that phone call, or the next two weeks. Dave had always made a point of letting us know how much he hated us. But just a couple of hours after he lost his mind on us at the coffee shop, he was calling to apologize, which was completely out of character for him. He said he was sorry that I had to witness that and he said I didn't deserve to see that. I was totally caught off guard by this because it was not his usual behavior.

Dave explained that he was angry because he did not feel like he was in control of our conversation in the coffee shop. He went on to say he knew everyone was worried about his risk level but told me not to worry. He told me he didn't feel like raping anyone.

I felt a cold chill run through my entire body and suddenly felt sick. Dave continued talking to me as I drove home and the whole conversation lasted for well over an hour.

I knew something was really wrong because he was talking to me and seemed like a completely different person. I'm not stupid and I figured he was trying to manipulate me somehow but I wasn't sure of his end game at this point. I don't think I would ever know what his end game was. This was the start of approximately two weeks of experiencing Dave in this way. In the long phone calls during this time period he told me all sorts of things I wish I'd never had to hear.

My job as a CCW was to provide support and supervision, so I listened when Dave wanted to talk. My only hope was that I might be able to prevent him from reoffending. In the end though, my efforts were a waste of time. Dave was caught up in his offence cycle and had no plans of letting us help him out of it. He filled my mind with poison during his phone calls and ended up reoffending anyways.

During those phone conversations, Dave told me about his addiction to pornography. He shared that he made $500 while working during the time he spent in jail and spent it all on pornography. He told me how angry he was that a judge ordered him not to access the internet. I told him there must have been a reason for it. That's when he shared the reason with me. Dave told me he was a "collector" and that Correctional Officers found his collection while he was in jail. He shared that he was collecting the names of women so he could look them up when he was released. He said he got the names by listening to the conversations of Correctional Officers and also from the newspaper. I believed this would become his victim pool for when he was released.

Dave was into performing magic and showed us a trick during one of our appointments. I hate to say it but he was very good at the trick he showed us. In one phone conversation he told me when his probation was finished he wanted to put on a magic show for all of us who worked with him. The very thought of it made me queasy and sent creepy chills down my spine.

During the time period of these phone calls with Dave, I grew more afraid each day. I kept most of this fear to myself. I had been working in a career where you couldn't show fear or feelings and I had learned it was best to keep them to myself. I knew he was a stalker (the guy even showed up to a team meeting wearing a shirt that said "stalker" on it). I became afraid that he might try to follow me. It was just a feeling I had and I think it was a game he enjoyed playing with me. I would look around everywhere before going to my car after work and I started locking both locks on the door of my house.

I remember one day when I dropped the work car off at the office. I pulled into the parking stall that was right in front of the office door, just as Dave was walking out of the building. He walked over to the car. I was on the phone but he stood there and waited for my call to be done so he could talk to me. I was alone in the car and it was one of the most uncomfortable feelings I ever had during my time as a CCW. After a very brief conversation with Dave I went inside the office to drop off the car keys and decided to hang around for a while. I was hoping Dave would be gone before I had to walk out to my own car. Maybe I was being paranoid but I knew what he was capable of. I was afraid and wanted to keep myself safe.

After a couple of weeks of these phone calls where he was sharing too much information, we were out doing curfew checks. Dave was home when we arrived. We usually called him when we got there and he would wave at us from his window because the building he lived in was too dangerous for us to enter. On this particular night he was in the window when we got there. He told us he knew we would be coming that night so he was waiting for us. Dave said we couldn't call him because he broke his phone. When I asked how he broke it, he told us he sat on it and it broke in half. It was an old flip phone so it might have been believable. It was just after midnight and he was our last curfew check of the night, so we left and were done with our shift.

It was fairly late by the time I got home and was able to get to sleep. And early the next morning I received a text message from one of the police officers who we worked with. His text said that Dave had reoffended in a very violent manner the previous night and they were going to arrest him at his workplace that morning. I felt sick when I read that message.

It turned out that Dave had arrived home from reoffending just minutes before we curfew checked him the previous night. He had grabbed a woman on a bridge, choked her unconscious and dragged her under the bridge where he planned to rape her. She woke up with him on top of her and started screaming so he ran. He didn't break his phone like he told us when we curfew checked him. In his rush to flee the crime scene, he dropped it and the victim picked it up and called 911. That's how Dave was caught. It was so hard to believe this was real. He appeared to be his usual self when we curfew checked him. In my mind's eye, I can still see his face in the window that night. I wondered how he could appear so calm after what he had just done.

It took a long time before I was able to put his most recent crime to the back of my mind where I hoped it would stay. But it didn't stay there. And neither did any of the other experiences I had while on the job.

***

I was suddenly jolted back to the present moment. The only feeling I had now was dread. How the hell was I going to get through testifying in court? This meant I could no longer keep Dave and his violent actions hidden in that part of my mind I had reserved for such things. I was terrified and my anxiety was through the roof. I felt like my world was spinning out of control and I had no idea how to stop it.

These traumatic incidents had a way of escaping from the part of my mind I had buried them in. In the beginning they escaped in the form of nightmares and then eventually into flashbacks where I had to relive them. And once they began escaping from the place I had them hidden, there was no stopping them. It was like watching a clown car. So many clowns pouring out with no end in sight and wondering how so many could possibly fit in such a small car. Turns out you can stuff a lot more in there than you ever imagined.

Chapter 5

Am I Dreaming?

The position of a Community Corrections Worker (CCW) was pretty demanding and required a lot of adjustments in my daily life. The position required me to work 6 days per week and answer my phone 16 hours a day. I was working exclusively with sex offenders, so no matter where I was or who I was with, I always had rapists and pedophiles with me.

They would call while I was at home, while I was in my bed trying to sleep, while I was in the grocery store, when I was driving, during walks with my dog, when I was on hikes, watching sunsets, taking photos and when I was with friends and family. They were ALWAYS with me. My phone didn't stop unless it was my one day off every week. And even then, I always thought I heard it ringing.

Working as a CCW meant you were never able to disengage from work unless you were sleeping. And when the nightmares started, it wasn't even possible to disengage during sleep.

One night during my last few weeks as a CCW, and just a couple of months after receiving the subpoena, I decided to go to bed early because I was exhausted. I hadn't been sleeping well due to the nightmares that were becoming a regular occurrence. One moment I was laying in my warm, comfortable bed and the next moment I'm with Jill and we are standing outside in the parking lot of McDonald's. I feel the warm morning sun shining on my face as George approaches us.

He starts the conversation by telling us he went out the previous night and was randomly driving around when he spotted a young girl walking down the street. He said she was visibly upset. He tells us he went and parked his vehicle a distance away and began walking towards her so he could "accidentally" bump into her.

He said when he approached her she was crying so he asked if she was okay and if she needed a ride anywhere. He told us she was very apprehensive about accepting a ride from him and asked him if anything bad would happen to her. "Only if you want something bad to happen" he says was his reply.

He tells us just as the girl is getting into his vehicle, the police pull up and start questioning him. He says they searched the inside of his vehicle. He was insulted by this because he claims he wasn't doing anything wrong. George tells us the police would not let him give the girl a ride anywhere. They found nothing in their search and let him go. This is disturbing because he is telling us this story like he's talking about the weather.

Was I asleep and dreaming? I didn't think so because this event had actually happened. I wasn't sure but I'm brought out of this moment by the ringing of my work phone. I answer it because I'm obligated to answer it until 1am. I am grateful for the interruption, but now I have to shake it off so I can talk to the client who is calling me. At the time this happened, I did not realize that what I had just experienced was a flashback.

***

I had some pretty vile and unpleasant clients during my time as a CCW. I describe them as vile because most of them lacked empathy. But George told me he didn't lack empathy. He straight up admitted that he had no empathy at all. Not for his victims and not for anyone.

Lacking empathy can make people dangerous. George had a history of raping very young girls who he claimed he thought were prostitutes. Now, even if you think someone is a prostitute, it does not give you the right to rape them. One of his victims was a pre-teen and could not have been mistaken for a prostitute. She was walking home from a sleepover, carrying a teddy bear when George grabbed her and stuffed her into his car. He drove into a back lane and parked his car with the passenger side against a building so she could not escape.

George was an extremely self absorbed individual and did nothing but either complain, or brag about how great he thought he was at every meeting we had with him. He constantly complained about each and every condition the court had imposed on him. And there were a lot of them. George did not think it was fair that he had so many conditions. He claimed he wanted to start his own business and that his conditions were holding him back from being successful. It was sickening listening to him constantly going on this way, so one day I asked George how he thought his victims were doing. He told me he's never thought about it. I told him I thought he lacked empathy and this is when George told me he didn't lack empathy and admitted to having none.

George had a job in the kitchen of a restaurant. He met a young girl who was also employed there. She was 19 years old and he was over 30. He was obsessed with this girl and talked about her all the time. He told us he wanted to ask her out but was worried she wouldn't be interested in him. He also told us he was thinking about telling her about his crimes and his time in prison. We strongly advised him against this. We also advised him to stay away from her, telling him he should find someone more age appropriate and not to get involved with people he works with.

One day he told us he talked to this young employee and told her that he was a high risk sex offender. He said she didn't seem shocked but was only interested in having a friendship with him. After divulging his criminal status he should have been grateful that she even continued working with him, let alone agreeing to have a friendship with him. And I'm sure that she was terrified and just trying to be nice by offering friendship so she wouldn't end up being one of his victims.

George had to abide by a curfew for the first year after his release from prison. When that first year was almost done, we cautioned him several times about going out without having any concrete plans. He told us he wasn't going to be doing that. But of course he did go out late at night and found who he thought would be his next victim. The girl that was upset and walking down the street that night he told us about.

The only reason George told us about that night was because he knew we would find out from the police what he had been up to that night. And we did. Turns out the police had been watching him as he was watching the young girl. They ran his license plate and discovered who he was so they decided to observe him. And good thing they did. Turns out when the police approached George's vehicle, the young girl silently mouthed the words "help me" to them. They literally saved her from becoming his next victim.

George thought he was being proactive by telling us what he had done that night. Too bad he wasn't also taking a proactive role in stopping himself from committing sexual offences.

Chapter 6

The Diagnosis

I knew what they were going to tell me that day I attended my follow up appointment at the University. They were going to confirm what I already knew. I have PTSD. I sat in that chair with my eyes focused on the report the psychologist held in his hand. The report that held my fate. I was afraid to make eye contact. Even though I knew what I was about to hear, I became very emotional when it was said out loud. There it was out in the open. It was real and it was hard to accept.

I was diagnosed with PTSD in early fall of 2018, just three months after I received that subpoena. For the longest time after that fateful day I was told I had PTSD, I kept thinking maybe it's not real. I'd been able to continue functioning what I thought was normally, so it can't be that bad. I thought that maybe I was imagining everything. Maybe the diagnosis was wrong. It happens to other people, not me. It was a hard thing to accept even though in my mind I already knew it was true. I was in denial. This might not make sense to you unless you've experienced something like it.

I had spoken to my boss shortly after receiving the subpoena when the nightmares and panic attacks started. She had suggested I contact our Employee Assistance Program (EAP). It was in late summer when I attended an appointment with an EAP counselor where I admitted to how I had been feeling. It was one of the most difficult things I've ever had to do. Admitting to struggling with my mental health was so hard because I had always been mentally strong. I had gotten through all the hard times and life's biggest challenges up until now on my own. Admitting to how much I was struggling made me feel weak.

After I explained what I had been experiencing, the counselor said it sounded like trauma and told me they didn't deal with that. I sat there for a moment, completely stunned. I felt like I had just been slapped in the face. I finally had the courage to disclose the things I had kept hidden and now I felt even more defeated by the counselor's reaction. Our EAP program was ready to send me back out into the world, traumatized and feeling even more defeated than I did when I arrived that day. They were ready to send me back out there to deal with this on my own. I was not offered any alternatives or suggestions on where to turn for help.

But I had come this far, so instead of just walking out, I asked what I was supposed to do now. I asked for resources or a referral to somewhere I could get some help. It was humiliating sitting there, asking for some kind of help when it should have been offered immediately. They might not deal with trauma but why weren't they offering alternative suggestions?

After asking for help, the EAP counselor told me about the University's psychology department. He told me their Masters students saw people free of charge. So I filled out all of the paperwork and sent it in. I got a response very quickly and scheduled an assessment appointment. The assessment was a series of tests as well as talking about some of the trauma I had experienced. After this appointment, I finally felt like I was on the right track.

In between the time I went for the initial assessment and the follow up appointment where I received the diagnosis, I had started a new job as a Probation Officer. I received my diagnosis about a week into my new position.

The day of that follow up appointment, a plan was devised for me. I would be able to see the student psychologist for a few months and it would take me through the trial I was to testify at. The trial that I received the dreaded subpoena for. I thought this sounded like a good plan, because at the time I had no idea how injured I actually was. I also thought it was good because I had just started a new job and was quite reluctant to let them know what I was facing because I was afraid it would taint their view of me.

So the following week I began seeing the student psychologist and I'm going to be brutally honest about this experience. It was extremely difficult, especially in the beginning, because I wasn't sure what I should disclose to her. It wasn't long before I started thinking I had made a huge mistake by asking for help. These sessions were not helpful at all because I was very reluctant to dive into details of my experiences with the student. I felt like she would never be able to understand my experiences and I was afraid of traumatizing her with the nightmares I had trapped in my head. I kept things on a superficial level with her and we focused mainly on my feelings around the upcoming trial I had received the subpoena for.

The way I was feeling had absolutely nothing to do with the student. She was kind, caring and a wonderful listener. I just felt like my injury was too much for a student to be dealing with and that I would be better suited seeing someone who had the expertise required for dealing with my specific type of traumas. But I didn't know where else to turn at the time because I did not want to go through Workers Compensation. So I got through the trial, continued working and kept seeing the student psychologist for a few more months. The whole time I still felt like I was on a downward spiral.

Chapter 7

Downward Spiral

I was up north, sitting in the office I saw clients in. I was going over the list of clients I had for the afternoon when another list popped into my mind's eye. It was the list of victims a previous client had written in his rape journal. The list was the names of all his victims, their ages and what he had done to them. I shook my head in hopes of making this mental picture disappear. But it did not disappear.

***

Sam is one of the worst offenders I have ever met. His distorted thinking made him extremely dangerous. I met Sam the day he was released from federal prison after serving 4 years for a variety of sexual offences against children.

Sam is a rapist and a pedophile. He would rape females of any age but had a preference for female children. Sam also had an addiction to crystal meth and when he started using again, made him even more dangerous.

Almost immediately after Sam was released from prison, he appealed the conditions of his release. He didn't like that he was not allowed to use the internet. He also did not like that he was ordered not to use drugs or alcohol. Sam did not think this was fair.

My work partner and I accompanied Sam to court the day his appeal was being brought before a judge. We had been discussing his addiction just minutes before he went into the courtroom. Sam told us that crystal meth is a very permissive drug that gives him permission to do anything he wants. It was terrifying that he thought this way, and equally terrifying that he was actually going to ask a judge to remove the condition that he not touch drugs or alcohol.

Sam was not a happy camper after his court appearance. His conditions were not going to be removed or changed in any way. He was also upset that the judge referred to him as a pedophile. He told us the judge used "the P word" and then told us he knows what he is and didn't appreciate the judge pointing it out.

Sam was only in the community for a few short months before he breached his court ordered conditions and was sent back to prison. In the short amount of time he was out, he had us shocked and disgusted on a regular basis.

Sam liked to talk about some of his offences and I think he did it for shock value. He would talk about it in very public settings with people in close proximity. I think he enjoyed seeing the reactions from the people around us. In a busy coffee shop one day, he explained and demonstrated how he watched little girls. He showed us how he hid behind his sunglasses and told us he had to do it that way because that sort of thing "is frowned upon by society". It was apparent that Sam didn't think there was anything wrong with his behavior.

Sam told us one day that he'd gone to see a movie with his mother. They went to see Logan. He told us it was really difficult to watch this movie with his mother because he was feeling extremely attracted to the girl in the movie. This girl was 12 years old when she played the part. He also shared this information with us in a crowded coffee shop.

One of the most disturbing things about Sam was his rape journal. It was honestly one of the most disturbing things I've ever read and I deeply regretted reading it. But I always felt that it was important to know exactly what my clients were capable of. And I couldn't write a proper safety plan with only part of the information. These safety plans we wrote were for our own benefit. They included detailed information so we knew exactly who we were dealing with, and so we knew how to keep ourselves safe while meeting with them in the community.

Driving home from work the day I read his rape journal gave me time to think about what I'd read. But I didn't want to think about it. I wanted it stuffed into that clown car, where I put every other disturbing and traumatic memory. I turned the music up really loud while I drove home, hoping that would drown out the thoughts. I even started singing but it didn't work. I drove into my garage and sat there in my car for a few minutes trying to shake off the thoughts and pull myself together before I entered my home. Somehow I thought if I could pull this off that I would be leaving work behind at the office. Of course I was very wrong about this.

Not only did Sam's rape journal have a list of his victims and how he sexually assaulted them, he also wrote his distorted views on the female gender. His misogynistic point of view was appalling and included his belief that girls should lose their virginity to their fathers by the age of 6. And if this isn't enough to disturb your mind, he also had a very young daughter.

Sam and his ex-girlfriend had a child together that they gave up for adoption. He told us one day that he'd been thinking a lot about his daughter. He told us if he had access to his daughter, it wouldn't have been a question of if he would have raped her. The only question would be when. I couldn't eat my lunch that day.

It should come as no surprise when I tell you that Sam had not been abiding by his court ordered conditions. He was using the internet to meet fellow pedophiles who shared his twisted views.

They were making plans for future victims. Sam was also using crystal meth again which made him extremely dangerous.

The day we heard Sam had been arrested and put back into jail for breaching his conditions was a relief. One more danger to the community was contained. But for every offender who went back to jail, another was released. It was a never ending cycle of rapists and pedophiles coming and going. Kind of like a freak show ferris wheel. Stopping at the bottom to release one rapist, while another one jumps on for the ride back to prison.

***

Once we were done working for the day, we returned to the cabins we called home for the weeks we spent up north. I had something to eat but could not shake the thoughts I'd had about Sam and his list earlier in the day. So I decided to go out for a walk in hopes of clearing my mind.

It was March and the weather was beautiful that day. It was the kind of day where there was still snow everywhere but it was melting and the air no longer had that cold bite that hurts your face. The sunset had just started and the sky was turning a beautiful shade of pink. It was a perfect evening for a walk.

As I walked down the long driveway towards the road, the local dog from the property started following me. I had seen this dog several times. He always greeted us when we arrived. He was young, friendly and always tried playing with the pom poms on my mukluks. On this particular evening, there was a second large dog on the property. I had never seen this dog before. He also started following, so the three of us set off down the road for a beautiful sunset walk.

About a kilometre into the walk, I decided to turn around and head back. I wanted to make sure I was back before it got dark. Just after we turned around, the dog who was unfamiliar to me was suddenly right beside me. He grabbed my mitt and started pulling it. He wouldn't let go. At first I thought he was trying to play with me. It was quite the struggle and he tore my mitt a bit, but I managed to get it back from him.

As soon as I got my mitt back he grabbed my right forearm with his mouth, held on tightly and would not let go. I was starting to feel a slow panic rise inside of me. This didn't feel playful at all. He was hurting me and I kept trying to pull my arm out of his jaws, but he was holding on and refused to let go. Talking to him was not working and my panic kept rising, so I tried kicking at him in hopes of distracting him so he would let my arm go, but it didn't work. I ended up punching him in the face because he was hurting me. He finally let go and I felt relieved. Until he attacked again.

This time he was behind me. He jumped up on my back and was biting my shoulder. I kept moving because I was afraid if I stopped it might be easier for him to knock me down because I think that's what he was trying to do. Suddenly, the friendly dog was behind me as well and he chased my attacker away.

But that didn't stop him for long. Once again he was behind me, jumping up on my back, trying to knock me to the ground. I was yelling at this dog and screaming for help. But there was no one out there to help me. I was completely alone on a deserted road, up north in a remote community.

The dog now had a very tight hold of my upper left arm and was not letting go. He was hurting me and I was terrified. I kept thinking I was going to die on that road that night. I also kept thinking that I couldn't let this dog knock me down because if he did, I would die for sure.

Once again I found myself yelling at this dog, kicking him and punching his face. It didn't seem to faze him one bit. And once again, the friendly dog came to my rescue and chased him away. I was slightly hysterical and crying by this point but I kept walking. All I could think about was getting back to the safety of my cabin.

After this latest round of attack, the dog started walking in front of me. I kept waiting for another attack but he just continued walking like nothing had happened. There was a point during these attacks when I had accidentally taken a step off the road in my efforts to escape being knocked to the ground. I remember my left leg sinking knee deep into the soft snow in the ditch. I was suddenly aware that my boot was full of snow but I couldn't really feel the cold at all. I couldn't risk stopping to get the snow out though. My only focus was on getting back to safety.

I finally arrived back at the cabins after what felt like an eternity. I was extremely distraught, shaking uncontrollably and afraid to be alone at that moment, so I knocked on my work partner's cabin door. I remember standing in her doorway shaking while she talked to me for a while until I felt calm enough to be alone. When I arrived back at my cabin, I took my boots off and realized there was still some snow in the left one. My leg was so cold to the touch and red but with all the adrenaline I had pumping through my body, I could not feel it.

Even though the weather had been very nice, I was wearing my thick winter jacket because the weather can change quickly in March and especially up north. That thick winter jacket saved me from being ripped to shreds by that dog's teeth. When I looked at my upper left arm, a bruise was already developing and there were teeth marks in the middle of it.

By the next day, I had purple bruises on both of my arms and my left shoulder. The bruise with teeth marks spread and spanned from my elbow to almost my armpit. My whole upper body was in a tremendous amount of pain and I was an emotional wreck. But I went to the office that day and met with all my clients. It was just another traumatic event that I would stuff into that clown car.

***

Things felt like they came to the breaking point for me after the dog attack. Within a few days of returning from up north, I very reluctantly submitted a claim to Workers Compensation. Seeing the student psychologist was not helping and things just kept feeling like they were getting progressively worse. I had resisted this route because I did not want to have to tell my employer that I had PTSD. Looking back now, it doesn't make sense, especially considering that my injury happened because of my work.

I felt a lot of shame at that time for not being able to handle things on my own. I tried my best to go it alone but some things are just too big and too much to handle alone. I will be forever grateful that I was finally able to recognize that I could not handle this on my own and that I was strong enough to ask for help.

Once I submitted my claim to Workers Compensation, I had no choice but to tell my new boss. I was nervous and afraid but soon realized I had nothing to fear. My boss did not react like my deepest fears had me believing he would. He listened without judgment and was very kind. The world could use a lot more people like him.

This new position I was in had me traveling approximately 800 kilometres up north every second week. It was a lot of work and a lot of time away from home but I was enjoying it. It was a small community. The nights were quiet and peaceful and I was far away from the places where I was exposed to the traumatic incidents that caused my injury. With the exception of the dog attack, I actually felt much safer when I was up north than I did when I was in the city I called home.

Within a couple of months of submitting my claim, I met the psychologist that Workers Compensation referred me to and my journey began. I saw my psychologist during the weeks I was back at home. I don't remember a lot from those early appointments but I do remember wondering how long therapy would take before I was recovered.

I was both extremely naive about the process and still in denial at the same time. I remember asking my psychologist how long it would take until I was better. He told me it would take as long as we needed it to take. I was confused and thought this was ridiculous. When you break a bone they tell you it takes about six to eight weeks to heal. So why wasn't I able to get a timeline for this injury?

It took a long time before I was able to understand what my psychologist meant. Everyone is different and no one's paths are the same. Hell, it took me at least a year before I even trusted my psychologist. And because I was in such denial, I didn't even realize at the time that I didn't trust him.

I kept working for a few months because I thought I could continue to work while doing the trauma recovery work. Another thing I didn't realize at the time is that it's not possible to recover while continuing to work in an environment where you are continually exposed to the very things that caused your injury.

Looking back now, that's pretty distorted thinking. All I did by continuing to work was prolong my recovery. I've said it before and I will say it again because it's important. You cannot recover while being in the same environment that caused your injury. And if you think you can, you're not ready to begin the real work of trauma recovery yet. I was not the exception to this. Once I was able to accept that, the real work began. That's also when my symptoms intensified and it felt like I began my descent into the depths of hell.

Chapter 8

Flashbacks

Those first few weeks I was away from work were not easy. I was accustomed to being constantly busy. The busier I was, the easier it was to keep all the traumatic memories locked away in that clown car. Suddenly I wasn't busy anymore and the lock on that car popped and the clowns started pouring out of there. These are not the happy clowns you expect to see. They are the scary clowns from the freak show my mind started replaying.

Early on in my recovery, I was sitting at home trying to make sense of everything that was happening in my life since I received my diagnosis and took time away from work. Abruptly, out of nowhere I could smell the jail and I felt like I was actually there.

Suddenly, there I was back in the jail, working a night shift and I am asked to accompany my supervisor to an inmate's cell. We are told he requested to talk to officers but we are not sure why. We approach the cell door and look inside. The inmate is sitting on the bunk so my supervisor signals for the door to be opened. The door is popped open by someone in the control pod so we enter the cell. The inmate is still sitting on the bunk and suddenly he jumps up and lunges at us, attacking my supervisor. I immediately call "code 33". The responders are there almost immediately.

There are five of us in this cell trying to restrain the inmate. He keeps fighting to be restrained. He is like a wild animal. We manage to get the handcuffs and shackles on him but he is still trying to fight. He keeps kicking even though he is shackled. The shackles are digging into his skin with every kick and he starts bleeding. I am standing on the chain between the shackles to keep him from hurting us and to hopefully stop the damage he is doing to himself. He is relentless though and keeps kicking. The shackles keep cutting deeper into the skin of his ankles, causing a bloody mess. It doesn't seem like he can feel pain.

The institutional medical staff on site can't do anything for him because he won't stop trying to fight his way out of the handcuffs and shackles. It's very clear he is in some kind of drug induced delusion. Someone called an ambulance.

The paramedics arrive and inform us they can not attend to someone who is uncooperative. They contact their supervisor for direction and then tell us if we can move him out of the cell, they will try to have a look at him.

We manage to carry this guy out of the cell and move him out of the range. It wasn't easy. He is extremely uncooperative and still trying to fight but he appears to be losing some steam. The paramedics are able to get close enough, and just in time. The inmate stops breathing. We are all standing there watching the paramedics revive him. It's quiet except for the paramedics talking to each other. It is surreal, is this really happening?

I'm suddenly brought back to the present moment but I don't feel like I'm in the present. I am shaken and feeling disoriented. I'm feeling the residual effects from the flashback. This wasn't a "normal" memory. I had just re-lived a very disturbing event. I felt like it had just happened in the now and not years ago. I tried to shake it off but I felt like I was going crazy. I was scared this would keep happening and I did not want to experience this again.

This would not be the only visual flashback I would experience. Visual flashbacks usually happen suddenly and uncontrollably. They feel like very vivid dreams. I can see, hear, smell and feel it like it's presently happening. Only it's not a dream. It's something I've already experienced and something I'm reliving while in flashback. It feels like it's happening all over again. The feelings that accompany visual flashbacks can be overwhelming. They can be terrifying because it feels like the event is currently happening and they leave you feeling exhausted and defeated. These can really do a number on your psyche.

***

In the early days of this journey, flashbacks were the norm. I hated when they happened. I wanted these events to stay where I buried them years ago. But they had a way of sneaking out and disrupting any semblance of a routine I had left. One scenario I thought I had forgotten about forever kept playing over and over in my mind like a movie. A very disturbing movie.

One night around 11pm, I got a phone call to come into work. I was told I would be going to the hospital as an inmate had just been taken out by ambulance. I was also told the inmate may not survive.

I arrived at the jail about an hour later and met my partner for the night. We left the jail and arrived at the hospital a short time later. We were not at all prepared for what we were about to witness. We were shown into the resuscitation room where the inmate was unconscious and had machines, tubes and hoses hooked up to him. We were told they had no idea what was wrong with him and that he was in critical condition. It was unsettling to say the least. I was so disturbed by what I was witnessing that I couldn't even drink the hot chocolate I had bought.

He was lying on the hospital bed and unconscious. There were hoses down his throat and he was attached to machines that were beeping. Abruptly, he sits up. His eyes are wide open and he starts pulling the hoses out of his throat and proceeds to spew green vomit all over the place. The nurses are quick to rush over and stop him from pulling out the IVs. He's laying down again and appears to settle back into unconsciousness.

After the incident where he pulled the hoses out of his throat, the medical team informed us they would be preparing him for transfer to another hospital. It took a while before he was ready to go. My work partner rode in the ambulance and I followed in the Corrections vehicle.

Once we got to the other hospital, the inmate was immediately put into quarantine as they had no idea what was happening with him. Once our relief arrived in the morning, we were told by the hospital staff they suspected the inmate may have meningitis. If that was the case, they informed us we would be required to come in for testing as we were in close proximity to him before he was quarantined.

I went home after that shift and had to get my daughter ready for school. I was afraid that if I had been exposed to meningitis or who knows what else, I could potentially pass it on to her. As I'm sure you can guess, sleep did not happen after that shift.

I worked again that night and when I arrived at work I found out the inmate did not have meningitis. He almost died because he drank antifreeze before being admitted into custody. It was a relief when I heard that he didn't have a contagious disease.

This inmate spent a couple of weeks in the hospital before returning to the jail. Upon his return, he laughed and bragged about how he almost died. I told him I knew that because I was there at the hospital that night. He continued to laugh. He seemed to find the situation funny, at least until I explained what we witnessed that night. Now if that was me who swallowed antifreeze, I'm sure I would not be here today to share this story with you.

***

A few nights later I was laying in bed hoping for sleep. Sleep was a serious problem at this time in my life. Suddenly I am transported through time again. I am working a night shift in the jail. We are exiting a cell where we just restrained an uncooperative female inmate. I hear a code being called for a medical emergency in the same area we are in. We respond immediately and there is a female inmate who is pregnant.

She is standing over the toilet with her baby hanging by the umbilical cord into the toilet bowl. She is hysterical. This sight is shocking and I literally stop breathing for a minute. The duty officer is on the phone with 911 and they are giving directions for what we should do until the paramedics arrive.

We are able to calm the inmate down a bit. We pick up the baby and wrap it in a towel and very slowly and carefully move the inmate and her baby over to the bed. The baby is only about twenty weeks along. The eyes are fused shut and the skin looks almost transparent. The legs are the size of my fingers. But the baby is alive and trying to suck on the corner of the towel.

We get the inmate to lay down on the lower bunk and we are told to find something to clamp the umbilical cord with. Being in a maximum security institution makes this almost impossible. We are about to use one of our boot laces when the inmate tells us to use her medicine bag. We use the string on the medicine bag to tie around and clamp the cord. The paramedics arrive just after we do this.

The baby is still alive, but not for long. At approximately 20 weeks, it most likely cannot survive as the lungs are not developed enough to make survival possible. A paramedic performs CPR with one finger. I'm watching this with tears in my eyes. I have never seen anything like this.

My dog jumps up on the bed and I'm jolted out of this flashback. I realize I'm safe and laying in my bed. I feel like this event just happened. I'm breathing too fast and if I can't slow it down I know I will have a panic attack. I try to distract myself with other thoughts but my mind is now only focused on that night so long ago. I start trying to take deep breaths but it feels like I can't, so I pick up my phone and start scrolling to try and distract myself.

I'm no longer in a flashback but I suddenly remembered what happened after the incident. Once we were finished with this incident there were reports to write and a debriefing to make sure everyone who was involved was okay. This took most of the night and when I returned to the area I was working in that night, my work partner complained that he was left to do all the work we normally shared.

We had just dealt with a horrifically traumatic incident that night and then I had to deal with a cold hearted, uncaring co-worker. Working in Corrections can be so demoralizing.

Chapter 9

The Realities of Working in a Prison

No amount of training can prepare you for the real world of working inside of a prison. When those heavy steel doors slam shut and lock behind you, you immediately feel like you've entered an alternate reality. And you have. The inside of a prison has its own culture and its own set of rules. And it's important to learn and understand that culture so you can survive while you're locked behind the doors. It's equally important to know that becoming immersed into, and understanding that culture will change you forever.

Most people will never know or be able to understand what it's like on the inside. After having worked on the inside, I'm pretty envious of those people. You see, working inside of a prison changes you. It will change the way you view the world. It will change the way you view yourself. And it will most likely change every relationship in your life. It might even feel like the job has stolen your soul. At least that's how it felt for me.

It's a thankless job. People with absolutely no clue what working with the criminal population entails will criticize and make assumptions about Correctional Officers for doing their jobs. Those people also have no idea what it feels like to walk into an inmate range alone where there are between 20 and 40 inmates wandering around, or what it's like dealing with people who can just turn on you at any second. People who are threatening to kill you and your family. People who are suicidal and absolutely desperate. People who are intoxicated on drugs and alcohol. People who are detoxing from drugs and alcohol. People who are experiencing psychosis. People who are combative and violent. People who are harming themselves. You are dealing with people who are at their absolute worst.

There are days where everything is predictable and goes well. But then there are the days where you find yourself in unsafe situations where nothing is predictable and anything can happen. Days where bad things can happen so fast it makes your head spin. Days where you find yourself confronted with violence and with no choice but to participate in that violence. These are the days that take the biggest toll on your mental health, whether you're willing to admit it or not.

It's not the kind of job that's easy to leave behind without another thought at the end of your shift. There are things you see and experience that can haunt your mind for days, weeks, months and even years afterward. Some shifts I used to say, "now I've seen everything". But there was always something else that would happen to make me realize that I hadn't actually seen everything, and probably never would.

It's definitely not a good career choice if you're squeamish. You will see things that you can't believe are real and you will see people doing things that shock you. There will be times you feel shaken to your core.

I've watched people drink from the toilet. I watched a guy wash his hair in the toilet bowl and I observed one guy urinate into a cup and then proceed to drink his own urine. I watched an inmate repetitively banging his head on a concrete wall until he was cut open and bleeding. I've seen inmates assault coworkers. I have seen copious amounts of violence and more pools of blood than I care to remember.

I have had to walk through toilet water and sewage after inmates flooded their range. I have seen people smear feces all over the walls as well as themselves. I have seen inmates saving their own urine and feces in pop bottles. They let this ferment and then shake up the bottle, put the opening end under another inmate's cell door and then stomp on it. This vile act is known as "shit blasting". This is the reality of the kinds of people you deal with when you are a Correctional Officer.

One time, I assisted a nurse who had to deliver a baby because it was making a very quick entrance into the world. And then a few hours later, I watched as CFS came and apprehended the baby. I felt heartbroken for that innocent little soul who had just entered the world.

One night shift, an uncooperative female inmate was admitted into custody. After behaving like a wild animal for half the night she was given a bag lunch, which consisted of a bologna sandwich. She took the bologna off the bread and made eye holes and a smiley mouth on it and stuck it to the window on the cell door. It was literally a bologna happy face. When we looked into the cell, she was crouched down in a squat position. When we asked what she was doing, she told us she was making a shit sandwich for us. She showed us the bread and she did, quite literally, make a shit sandwich. We laughed, not because it was actually funny. But because we used humor as a coping mechanism.

You can leave the jail, but the jail doesn't leave you. It's been 10 years since I worked behind the walls and sometimes I can still hear those heavy steel doors slamming shut. Or the clicking sound of handcuffs being tightened onto someone's wrists. Sometimes I can still smell that familiar combination of body odour, cheap laundry detergent, Mr. Noodles and Irish Spring soap.

A lot of Correctional Officers end up hanging out together because of the job. It helps to have friends that understand and know exactly what you deal with at work. We deal with a lot of traumatic stuff that most people cannot comprehend. Sometimes you can tell a friend something that happened at work and they'll just stare at you, not knowing what to say. You learn pretty quickly that certain things should be kept to yourself. So hanging out with coworkers helps you feel less alone. Because after a few years on the job, it can sometimes feel like you have nothing in common with your old friends.

It's important to maintain those other friendships though. It's important to not make your entire life about the career. Because at the end of the day, it is just a job. A job where they don't really care about what happens to you. A job that will have you replaced five minutes after you're gone.

***

It's not just the inmates that make working in jail a difficult job. Some of the people you have to work with can make you question whether you should ever trust another living soul again.

There was one gal who came to work at the jail about a year after I started. She was assigned to work in the same unit as me. Her name was Nadia and she seemed very nice, friendly and easy to talk to, so another coworker and I became fast friends with her. It turned out to be a huge mistake.

There is no way we could have possibly known it at the time, but Nadia was having a very inappropriate relationship with one of the inmates in our unit. When I found out about it, it was shocking to say the least. She was living a double life. One of those lives was as a Correctional Officer and the other life was as the girlfriend of a very dangerous offender.

The inmate she was in a relationship with was known for dozens of armed robberies. Not only was she in a relationship with this inmate, she was also telling him personal information we had shared with her. Once I found out about her involvement with this inmate, I was able to look back and see that there were signs of what she was up to.

One day at work she asked me and another coworker which inmate we would choose to have sex with. We were surprised with this inappropriate question and quickly told her none of them. She asked again but worded it a bit differently. She asked which one we would pick if we had to choose one. Again we both told her we wouldn't choose and we didn't like the game she was playing.

Nadia had also been asking us to switch shifts with her. She claimed to enjoy working evenings and weekend shifts. I traded a few shifts with her because it was always nice to have a weekend off. But once her dirty deeds were revealed we knew why she preferred evening and weekend shifts. Less management in the building to observe what she was up to.

The inmate she was involved with had started to become overly friendly with us. It seemed strange but so much about working there was strange, so I didn't really question it. I just assumed he was probably trying to manipulate us for some reason. Once their relationship became known, I understood his behaviour towards us. She had been sharing information with him. In his mind, we were friends with his girlfriend. It was so disturbing and we had to assume that he was told everything we shared with her.

This situation had me questioning myself and how I could have trusted her. When I look back now, I realize I did nothing wrong by trusting her. And the only thing I should have been questioning was her lack of proper judgement and using co-workers for her personal gain.

Nadia was fired from the job right after she was caught. Shortly afterwards, I heard she had applied for a job with an armoured car company. To help her boyfriend with his next robbery, no doubt.

***

There were other people who worked in the jail that could make your shift a living hell. The ones who were confrontational with inmates and looking for fights. And others who made you question what the hell was wrong with humanity. The amount of bullying I witnessed and experienced surpassed anything that happened in high school. It could be an extremely toxic environment depending on who you were working with.

When I think of workplace bullying, there are a handful of people who come to mind. I showed up for a shift one day and one of my male co-workers looked me up and down and said "I see they only sent me half a guard to work with today". I was fairly new on the job and I found this shocking. I wasn't sure if he was referring to my size or the fact that I was a woman.

One of the first things I discovered when I began my career in Corrections is that a few of my male co-workers had issues with women working in the jail and were very open about it. To this day I still wonder why they thought that way, especially when the jail housed female inmates as well. Who did they think was going to perform all the strip searches on those women?

One male coworker shared with me what he felt the hiring process for Correctional Officers should be. He explained that you should have to get in a ring and fight the biggest, worst inmate and if you won the fight then you get hired. Not only is this way of thinking completely distorted, it's absolutely ridiculous. Violence happens in jails for sure, however, the role of a Correctional Officer is quite the opposite. We were there to prevent violence, not perpetrate it.

If you made it known that you found some situations disturbing, the toxic people would tell you that you need to "suck it up" and "grow thicker skin". That's the worst advice you can ever give to another person. When you feel like you can't talk about something you find disturbing, you're forced to keep it inside. Is it any wonder why so many people in this career end up with PTSD?

There were also a lot of incredible people who I worked with in the jail. A few of those people have become my very good friends and remain so to this day. These are the people who helped get me through some of the worst experiences I had while working in the jail. I will be forever grateful for these amazing souls and our continued friendship.

Chapter 10

You Can't Reason With a Psychopath

The flashbacks I was experiencing around this time in my journey were relentless. I felt like I was reliving every traumatic memory I had. I was afraid to close my eyes. I was afraid to go to sleep. I was afraid to be alone with my thoughts but I was more afraid of talking to people about those thoughts. Isolation felt like the safest option at the time.

Being alone with the frequent flashbacks kept me falling down into that dark hole. And just when I would crawl my way to the top of that hole, another flashback would come along and knock me down there again. It was exhausting and some days it felt easier to just stay down there.

***

I am sitting in our work vehicle with my partner Jill and he's in the backseat. Even though the early evening sun makes the vehicle feel warm, there is a cold chill throughout my body. His hands are clenched tightly into fists. He is seething with anger, his face is red and he is not speaking. This is very uncomfortable and borderline terrifying.

I'm starting to feel very afraid. I picture Dean reaching into the front seat and wrapping his large hands around our throats. I try to stop the mental pictures playing in my mind but it is difficult. I keep thinking about what I read in his criminal profile about him having rape revenge fantasies about women who he thinks have wronged him.

He finally starts to speak. Dean is furious with the police for curfew checking him. He is angry because he does not approve of their methods for gaining entry to his building. He is being completely unreasonable and acting entitled, which is his usual behavior. He doesn't seem to realize that the reason for the curfew checks is his own doing. Dean is a convicted rapist and murderer but he thinks he should be calling the shots here.

We try to reason with him but it doesn't appear to be working. It's pretty much impossible to reason with a psychopath. We try to change the subject and talk about his new girlfriend. He relaxes his fists slightly and starts talking about her. He tells us she is a virgin and he doesn't know how to talk to her about his sexual preferences. We go with this conversation because he's less upset now. We give him some advice and try to conclude the meeting. He's calmed down a bit more and finally gets out of the vehicle.

I almost feel like I can breathe now. I didn't realize I had been holding my breath so much. Jill and I look at each other in disbelief and she asks me if I was afraid. I tell her I was terrified and then I'm back in my living room. I am breathing too fast but I know I am safe.

***

Dean's criminal offences are like something straight out of a horror movie. He is a sexual sadist and a psychopath, so he cannot feel empathy.

Dean had a plan to kill all of his family members. He was caught after he murdered the first one. The family member he murdered was an older female. After he killed her, he violated her dead body by raping her and sexually assaulting her with a knife. He also killed her dog. Dean then hung out in her house for a few days, eating all the food in the fridge and playing video games. He did all this while his dead family member was tucked away in a closet.

Dean spent only a few short years in prison before being released with very strict conditions. Conditions he did nothing but complain about constantly. He hated the police, he hated us and it seemed that he basically hated the entire world.

Reading through Dean's criminal profile was a disturbing experience. He had sexual preferences that were violent, and rape revenge fantasies about women he felt had wronged him. Dean was extremely self entitled and complained every time we met with him about how unfair his court ordered conditions were. He hated being curfew checked and complained about it every chance he got.

Dean was court ordered to see a psychologist. He complained about having to do this as well. He told us it was not helpful. He said it was a waste of time because he got nothing out of attending therapy.

Dean used to complain to us on a regular basis about his family. He was angry with his brother, because his brother would not let him see his niece. Instead of thinking his brother had a very good reason for denying him access to his niece, he was offended by this. I can't say I blame the brother considering Dean's plan was to murder his entire family.

I had to mentally prepare myself whenever we met with Dean. He was extremely negative and his views about everything were pretty warped. He would complain every time I said something positive. He looked at Jill one day and asked her how she could stand being around me because I always had something positive to say. It was the first time I had ever heard someone complaining about positivity.

Dean had a job dealing with the public in retail for a while before he eventually went back to school. Be careful out there, because you never know who's sitting next to you in class or who is selling you a new watch.

Somehow Dean managed to get a girlfriend. A young girl with a religious background whom he told us was a virgin. She had no idea that Dean was a murderer, a rapist, a psychopath and sexual sadist. She had no idea what he was capable of and we were not allowed to tell her. His court order expired before their relationship ended so we have no idea how that played out. But I'm sure it didn't end well.

Chapter 11

Eye Movement Desensitization & Reprocessing (EMDR)

About 10 months after I started seeing my psychologist, Covid shut down the world and left me more isolated than ever. It was months before I would be able to see my psychologist in person again, so in the meantime the appointments were over the phone. And I'm sure I don't need to tell you that therapy over the phone is just not the same. We had talked about doing a type of therapy called Eye Movement Desensitization & Reprocessing (EMDR) before everything closed down, but that would have to wait.

A few months later I was able to resume seeing my psychologist in person. And it was right around this time I realized that I hadn't really been able to open up completely and trust him the way I would need to for therapy to be effective. Realizing this was when things started to change for me. I was almost ready to try EMDR.

***

We are parked in front of his building after arriving a few minutes early for our meeting. It's a shabby looking building in a bad neighbourhood. To our surprise he is in front of his building throwing some garbage and a chair into the bin. He spots us and waits for us to get out of the vehicle. Jill and I look at each other and know exactly what the other is thinking. I hope he's not throwing away all that stuff to make room upstairs to keep us confined.

We get out of the car and follow him up the dimly lit staircase to his apartment. The stairs are creaking, the walls are dingy and have graffiti on them and there is paint peeling away. Reluctantly, we follow him inside the suite. There is nothing nice about this tiny apartment but it is pretty neatly organized. It reminds me of how inmates keep their jail cells, but then I'm assuming that spending 12 years in prison taught him how to organize things this way.

There is a tiny black kitten running around. It's playful and cute but we can't let this distract us from the murderer/rapist in our presence. Kevin is socially awkward so it's hard to have a proper conversation with him at this point. We talk about the kitten and then try to set up the voicemail on his telephone while he watches us.

We leave the suite and can't get down the stairs and out the door fast enough. I hear a voice telling me that I'm safe. I realize I'm with my psychologist and this was what came up during an EMDR session. I'm starting to panic so the EMDR session stops.

***

Kevin had spent 12 years in prison for murdering his wife. He also raped her friend and tied her up with an extension cord in the house he lived in. He did all of this while his children were asleep in their beds. The first time I met Kevin was the day he was being released from prison.

He had some people fooled with the lies he told but I always felt like something was off with Kevin. He made it appear that he had reintegrated himself back into society with ease and without much help. This was my first warning sign that not all was well with Kevin. He told us he had a job, that he wasn't hanging out with any of his old criminal friends and that he was staying sober. We would come to find out that none of this was true.

I had been skeptical about Kevin since the beginning. At the time, I was partnered up with a newly graduated Social Worker who was in the role of a Probation Officer. Linn was filling in for the regular probation officer I worked with, who was away on maternity leave. Linn believed everything Kevin told her.

I told Linn that Kevin did not show up for a community meeting with us, and that we spotted him staggering through a parking lot about an hour after our meeting was supposed to take place. I explained that we stopped and spoke to him and he appeared intoxicated. He claimed he forgot he was supposed to meet with us. Linn told me that Kevin was not intoxicated because he didn't drink or do any drugs. Working with this woman was extremely difficult because she knew nothing about the realities of working with the criminal population.

Later that week we did a curfew check on Kevin and he was not at home. We reported this to the police and a warrant for his arrest was issued. Kevin was arrested and taken back to jail, but he wouldn't be there for long.

Linn advocated to have Kevin released from custody. People were shocked. We worked with extremely high risk offenders so this was unheard of. She wanted to give Kevin a chance because she believed every word that came out of his mouth. All of them were lies.

So with Linn's help, Kevin was released back into the community. According to him, being out after curfew was all a misunderstanding. Until it happened again. Shortly after his release, Kevin had breached his curfew again. Another arrest warrant was issued and he knew it, so he went on the run.

While he was on the run, Linn told us we had to go to his apartment and get his kitten. This seemed to be her biggest worry at the time and she seemed to think that the Department of Justice was responsible for rescuing that kitten. This kitten seemed to be more important than the colossal mistake she made by advocating for Kevin to be released and putting us in this current situation. Not to mention putting the public at risk by advocating for his release. We told her the protocol was when someone had a warrant for their arrest, we were not supposed to see them. She told us she didn't think he was dangerous and that she had contacted the landlord to let us into his suite to get the kitten.

We went to his building and spoke with the building manager. We told him we were not going to enter the suite because we had no idea if Kevin might be hiding in there. So the building manager entered the suite and brought the kitten out to us. Don't get me wrong, I'm happy to have saved that kitten. I just didn't appreciate being put in a dangerous situation by an extremely inexperienced coworker. This would also not be the only dangerous situation Linn put us in.

With Kevin on the run, the police were out several times searching for him. When they finally caught up with him, he gave the police quite the chase before he was apprehended. He was carrying a large knife at the time of his arrest. He was also intoxicated on crystal meth. None of this would have happened if Linn did not advocate for his release the first time he breached his court order. Thankfully no one was hurt.

Kevin was finally back in custody where he belonged. In a meeting with the police, we were told that Kevin came clean with them and told the truth about everything. He did not have a job. He had only worked temporarily for a few hours one day. He admitted to hanging out with his criminal buddies and was doing everything illegal that they were doing. He admitted to using crystal meth and supplying it to various women in exchange for sex.

Kevin called me from jail, looking for sympathy. He told me the police beat him up, because they all told me that. I told him I had zero sympathy for him and that there was nothing I could do to help him before I hung up the phone.

I had always had an uneasy feeling whenever I was in Kevin's presence and now I knew exactly why. His vibes and his stories didn't match up. I would put this latest incident in that clown car, where I stuffed all the things I never wanted to remember. And this one stayed there until that EMDR session that day in my psychologist's office.

***

Eye Movement Desensitization & Reprocessing (EMDR) was rough, but worth it. It's not something you can do when you first start therapy. It took some time and preparation before I was ready to try it.

At the beginning of this journey, it was all about learning to trust and feel safe with my psychologist. It was about learning how to breathe through panic attacks and learning grounding techniques. It was learning to visualize a place where I felt safe, and learning how to keep myself in the present moment. Once those things were mastered, I was able to start digging deep and be completely honest with myself.

It might sound easy, but this was extremely hard work to do and I'm not going to pretend it wasn't. It was the hardest work I've ever had to do in my life but completely worth it. In those early days of therapy I felt utterly lost, like I was fumbling through my days. Pretending to the outside world that I was not as hurt as I was. And the truth is, at that point I really didn't understand the depth of my injury yet. It wasn't until I began making progress that I started to see just how injured I was and how it ultimately affected every single part of my life.

After learning the skills I would need to cope on my own, I was ready to begin Eye Movement Desensitization & Reprocessing (EMDR). This therapy was done with my psychologist. It's basically just following a back and forth movement with your eyes while thinking of a traumatic memory. My eyes followed as my psychologist waved his fingers back and forth for the process while he guided me on what to think about. This sounds very simple, however, there is nothing simple about the emotions that are brought up during an EMDR session.

Once he stopped waving his fingers, he would ask what thoughts came up. I would tell him what came up and then he starts waving his fingers again while I'm thinking about that new thought. And again something different comes up. The process is repeated a few times each session. It was amazing the things that were coming up for me. It seemed kind of random but there's nothing random about trauma. Everything is connected. And you learn that through therapy. It was also very common for me to have panic attacks during these sessions.

I was completely exhausted after each EMDR session and that's to be expected. There are times I arrived at home without any recollection of driving there. Processing traumatic memories is exhausting so it was important to get lots of rest afterwards. I didn't make any kind of plans for the day of, or the day after these sessions.

The EMDR helped quite a bit and I am grateful for the experience. There are a few traumatic memories I have that don't evoke the same feelings or responses they once did. While EMDR was helpful, it's not magic. It was simply one of the tools I was able to use to help in my recovery.

In the beginning of this journey, I was naive. I thought that after a few months of therapy I would be healed and ready to get back to work. That wasn't the case at all. In the beginning I had no idea just how much work is required for recovery to happen. It takes a lot more than talk therapy to reach the stage of post traumatic growth.

Chapter 12

Realistic Recovery

Recovery from trauma isn't about reaching an end goal. It's a lifelong journey of growth and self improvement. Realistic recovery is a lot of work that doesn't end once you walk out of your psychologist's office. Therapy is there to help you learn, grow and gather the tools you will need to continue the recovery path on your own.

Realistic recovery is knowing you will never be your old self again. It is being committed to improving yourself and becoming a better version of yourself. It's about learning what your triggers are and eventually how to manage those triggers.

Triggers happen and they can happen unexpectedly just about anywhere. Triggers can be caused by sights, sounds, smells, places, movies, television shows, the news, the dates on the calendar, a season or anything that reminds our nervous systems of previous traumatic events. Learning what my triggers were and how to manage those triggers has been one of the most challenging parts of this journey.

I did a lot of reading in the earlier days of my journey and one of the most important things I learned is that trauma is not all in our minds. It is stored in our nervous systems. Our bodies remember traumatic events and how we responded during those moments. When we are triggered, it's our nervous system reacting to what it remembers as something threatening.

When I'm triggered or feeling anxious, I know that it doesn't always make sense for the current situation I'm in, but knowing that doesn't make the anxiety disappear. The moment I'm triggered by something, it really feels like I have no control over my reaction. And after the perceived threat has passed, I usually feel embarrassed and ashamed about how I reacted. It can be a vicious cycle. Learning to manage trigger responses is difficult but not impossible. I'm still learning and growing through the recovery process and I'm getting better at it every day.

Realistic recovery takes a lot more than talk therapy and pharmaceutical medication. If your recovery plan only includes these two things, you're only doing half the work. Nobody really tells you this though. It's very important to find a therapist who is knowledgeable in all the ways trauma affects the mind and the body.

Remember when I mentioned that some people are deemed to have "treatment resistant" PTSD? I have a huge problem with this because I did not take medication and CBT did not work for me, so I suppose I was "treatment resistant". After going through this process, I don't believe in "treatment resistant" PTSD. I believe that realistic recovery includes a lot more than taking medication and having a therapist use Cognitive Behavioural Therapy (CBT) with you. I believe that only using CBT and medication is the problem and not that people are "treatment resistant". I believe trying non-conventional methods to treat PTSD can lead to more success. I believe this to be true because this was the case for me.

Thinking you are treatment resistant can make you feel like you will never recover. It might make you feel like a failure. You are not a failure. You just haven't discovered what works for you yet.

I'm not saying that CBT is bad. It's definitely a good type of therapy. It just is not effective when used for post traumatic injuries. Trauma needs to be processed and that cannot be done through the use of CBT.

***

The goal of CBT is to help people understand how their thoughts impact their actions. There are three main pillars to it which are identification, recognition and management.

The first pillar is identification. This is when you identify your thoughts, behavior and emotions. You cannot change what you are not able to identify. And trauma survivors can have a great deal of trouble trying to identify emotions, especially in the beginning.

A simple example of identification would be noticing that you have a lot of negative thoughts around a specific thing, event or person. Once you are able to identify your negative thoughts, the next step is learning to recognize when those thoughts pop up.

The second pillar is recognition and it seems pretty similar to identification. Recognition is not just identifying that you have negative thoughts, but noticing the thoughts while they're happening. Once you're able to recognize that you're thinking or behaving in a negative way, you're able to stop it.

Management is the third pillar. It involves using skills and activities you've learned to help ease your mind of the negative thoughts. Management can be done in the moments of recognition and also outside of those moments. Management involves practicing the skills you've learned during all the moments in your life, both the good and the bad, to ensure that you'll be able to use them when the negativity returns.

Sounds pretty simple right? This type of therapy can work wonders for some things. But it does not help to process trauma, and trauma informed therapists will know this. When this therapy doesn't work (and it won't) for your post traumatic injury, you will be deemed "treatment resistant". Let's take a look at why this therapy doesn't work for post traumatic injuries.

Trauma is not just about your thoughts. Let me repeat that. Trauma is not just about your thoughts. Trauma affects your entire being. Traumatic events are stored in the nervous system. This is why when you are triggered by something, you have a hard time controlling your reaction. All the CBT in the world cannot fix this because the reaction comes from your nervous system, not your thoughts.

Learning to control trigger reactions comes from doing nervous system work. Combining nervous system work with CBT can be beneficial. But you're not going to gain control over your trigger responses by using CBT alone. Once you are able to relax your nervous system, you will be able to start understanding and identifying your triggers easier. And once you understand your triggers, CBT can be used to help with recognizing and controlling your reactions to those triggers. You are not "treatment resistant", your recovery plan just needs to be adjusted to add activities that are beneficial in calming your nervous system.

Chapter 13

The Nervous System's Role in Trauma

I'm definitely no expert on the nervous system. I'm just someone who has experienced a post traumatic injury that has affected not only my mind, but my nervous system as well. Once I started working on ways to calm my nervous system, things began to change for me in a big way.

Our nervous systems are pretty complex. I'm not going to go too in-depth on this topic but it is important to understand the basics as it relates to experiencing trauma.

Trauma is defined as anything you go through that brings up strong associative emotions after exposure to an emotionally disturbing event or a life threatening incident. The nervous system remembers how you felt at that time and associates that feeling with the memory and tucks it away in the dark parts of our mind. Not only does trauma interrupt our nervous systems normal functioning by dysregulating it, trauma can also disrupt a person's ability to cope and this impacts everyday functioning. Once I learned about the impact trauma has on our nervous systems, it was a game changer for me. And now I hope it can be a game changer for you as well.

When the nervous system is regulated, it will experience stress and calming throughout the day. Think of being in traffic. Maybe you just had someone in the lane next to you start to come over into your lane. You swerve to avoid being hit and avert the crisis. When your nervous system is regulated you will feel some stress in this situation. Once your body is feeling safe again your nervous system will calm down and go back to its original physiological baseline.

The same can be said when you are running late for work or an appointment. Your nervous system will feel the stress of you rushing to get there on time. Once you arrive on time, your nervous system relaxes back to its baseline and you feel calmer.

Now let's look at what happens when trauma affects your nervous system. Traumatic incidents push the nervous system beyond the ability to regulate itself. When a stressful situation pushes the nervous system past its limits, it can become stuck in fight or flight mode. When we get stuck, we may experience anxiety, panic, hyperactivity and possibly anger.

After a traumatic experience, some nervous systems will stay like this. Others may dip below this and become stuck. This is when we may become depressed, disconnected and exhausted.

Dr. Dan Siegel came up with the term "window of tolerance". The window of tolerance is when life feels comfortable and we can regulate ourselves without much effort after a stressful event. Trauma causes us to lose that ability and so the window of tolerance becomes very narrow, making it extremely difficult for our nervous system to get back to its baseline.

Now let's discuss the brain's role in a traumatic situation. Trauma actually rewires the brain. When our brains get stuck in stress, it physically changes the brain and causes symptoms that are life altering.

I'm sure you've heard the term "shake it off". This term comes from the world of animals. When an animal experiences trauma, they will shake it off, literally, which helps the animal get rid of the energy from the traumatic experience.

The same can be said for the term "shaking like a leaf". This term is used to describe a reaction to a scary situation. Shaking and trembling comes from the limbic brain which is the part of the brain that holds emotions. The shaking or trembling sends a message that the danger is over and that the fight/flight system can go back to normal.

Animals can die if they are unable to shake off the traumatic experience. Human beings can also shake off traumatic events, but in some cases that response isn't available at the time and this is when trauma is stored in the body. In humans, not being able to shake it off may turn it into a mental or physical condition. When this happens, it can lead to PTSD.

After a traumatic incident that represents a threat to our personal safety, the brain and body are transformed. This threat activates our Sympathetic Nervous System (SNS) and is known as fight or flight. After a traumatic experience, the SNS stays activated which keeps the mind and body on high alert, watching for signs of danger everywhere. Or what is referred to as hyper vigilance.

When the nervous system and brain become stuck on high alert, it makes healing from the experience a challenge. The late neuroscientist Paul MacLean, said the brain is made up of three parts and those parts are as follows:

1) The reptilian brain consists of the brainstem and cerebellum. This is responsible for survival instincts such as eating, sleeping, waking, heart rate and breathing.

2) The mammalian brain or limbic/midbrain is involved in monitoring danger, nonverbal memory and processing emotions.

3) Neo-mammalian brain, or thinking brain, consists of the frontal cortex which is in the outer area of the brain and surrounds the limbic system. It is required for conscious thought, learning, memory, self awareness and verbal expression.

During a traumatic experience, the reptilian brain is activated. It alerts the body to react and go into survival mode. This is when the SNS prepares itself for fight or flight. In situations that are not life threatening, the brain and body are able to soften this reaction and shift back to its normal baseline.

When trauma happens, the stress and hormones activated in the brain are stuck in survival mode and do not restore themselves. The reptilian brain stays in this state of looking for threats which keeps a person in this reactive state, which effects other parts of the brain to react accordingly. If your brain is constantly in this stress mode, it will flow down and become normalized by the physical body, which also normalizes the behaviour. When the brain does not reset itself, PTSD can develop. These are biological and chemical changes in the brain, which can change reality as you knew it. It is, indeed, an injury.

When your life is impacted by trauma, it can be shocking to your entire being. You may not feel like the same person you were before the traumatic experience. You may feel like you've lost control of your mind and body. Things begin to feel overwhelming and when the brain becomes dysregulated, the following chemical imbalances happen:

1) The amygdala becomes overstimulated. The amygdala is responsible for survival and threat related identification, as well as applying memories with emotion. After a traumatic experience, the amygdala can become caught up in a highly alert and activated loop where it looks for and perceives threats, literally everywhere.

2) The hippocampus, which is involved with learning and memory, becomes under active. Increases in the stress hormone, glu-

cocorticoid, kills cells in the hippocampus. This interruption will keep the mind and body stimulated in a reactive mode, as neither element receives the message that the threat has passed. This is the part of the brain where triggers may be stored.

3) A constant elevation of stress hormones that interfere with the body's ability to regulate itself. The SNS remains highly activated which leads to exhaustion of the body and many of its systems. When the brain deals with trauma this way, intense symptoms may develop.

I hope this very basic explanation helps you to understand the huge part our nervous systems play in traumatic experiences. It's not all in our heads and that's why recovery requires so much more than just Cognitive Behavioural Therapy and medication.

Trauma dysregulates the nervous system and this is why you may be stuck in fight or flight mode. If you still think PTSD is all in your mind, ask yourself if any of the following things apply to you:

Do you always feel on edge? Is it hard for you to relax?

Do you often feel anxious or stressed out?

Do you have difficulty falling asleep or staying asleep?

Do you have any issues with your digestive system such as IBS or diarrhea?

Do you struggle with controlling your moods and emotions? Are you frequently irritable?

Do you suffer from chronic pain such as migraines, neck pain, nerve or joint pain or fibromyalgia?

Do you have trouble with focus or concentration?

If you answered yes to these questions, your nervous system may be dysregulated. It sucks, I know. But there is hope and there are activities you can do to help calm your nervous system and get it back to a regular baseline.

Chapter 14

My Recovery Plan

I'm not suggesting that my recovery plan will work for anyone other than myself. There is no one size fits all in trauma recovery. Everyone is unique and so is each recovery plan. I am simply sharing with you what has worked for me so you can see there is so much more to recovery than therapy and medication. Maybe you already know this, or maybe you're just hearing this for the first time. Bottom line is, everyone is different and everyone's recovery will look different as well.

The following activities are some of the things that have helped me bring my nervous system back to a somewhat regular baseline. These activities have been proven to help calm your nervous system and get you on the path towards post traumatic growth.

Yoga

When you think about yoga, you may be rolling your eyes and thinking about a popular exercise class and wearing trendy yoga attire. Today in North America, yoga is known as a popular workout rather than a practice of one of the oldest rituals known to man. In today's North American culture yoga is simply a type of exercise. But it is so much more than that.

The practice of yoga dates back over 5000 years. The original purpose of yoga was for spiritual development and to learn to observe and become aware of the mind/body connection. The purposes of yoga were to cultivate self discovery, awareness, self-regulation and higher consciousness.

The development of yoga is aligned with the rise of Eastern spirituality and before the political power of religion that we see today. Yoga was seen as a method of a direct connection with the Divine. The very foundation of yoga is a spirit/body connection. The word "yoga" is the Sanskrit word for "union". Yoga is the longest lasting spiritual practice going on today, however, you don't have to believe in anything or be a spiritual person to enjoy the benefits of practicing yoga.

In addition to being a spiritual practice, yoga is very beneficial for helping to regulate your nervous system. It's one of the best ways I have found to keep my nervous system in a more relaxed state. There are many different types of yoga, however my focus will be on Kundalini yoga as that's what I practice and have found to be the most effective for myself.

Kundalini yoga is known as the "yoga of awareness" and has an interesting history. I won't go into details about the history, other than to say if it weren't for Yogi Bhajan coming to North America in 1968, Kundalini yoga would most likely still be unknown on this continent.

There is no philosophy that has been more lasting than Kundalini yoga. The objective has always been for people to get in touch with their higher selves. Kundalini yoga does not hold onto any religious beliefs and allows people to find their own personal meaning in the practice.

Kundalini yoga uses a unique combination of movement, breath work, mantra and meditation. All of these things can help calm an overstimulated nervous system. It can also help improve general well being and lead to a sense of ease and peace.

In our North American culture, people tend to look for a quick fix and pills are pushed on us as a means to cope with unwanted symptoms. For a lot of people, it's not likely that they would consider something as simple as yoga to be helpful with the symptoms of anxiety and depression. Oftentimes when we are in the darkest of places and feeling desperate to feel better is when we might consider some unconventional methods in hopes of feeling better. This was the case for me and I did not realize how important yoga would become in my recovery and my life in general.

When I first learned that yoga could be beneficial for trauma recovery, I tried a couple of different types like Vinyasa and Hatha yoga. It wasn't until I tried Kundalini yoga that I started to feel improvements. Kundalini yoga literally changed my life.

The first few times I practiced, the kriya included Plow Pose. This inverted pose helps to rejuvenate the entire nervous system. After this pose was the relaxation period. During this period of relaxation, I couldn't stop the tears from flowing. I knew it was helping to release some of the trauma that was stuck in my nervous system. It was an amazing experience.

I had chronic neck, shoulder and back pain for years which I thought was the result of a car accident I had been involved in. This chronic pain would often lead to debilitating migraines that would last for days. Turns out this chronic pain was not a result of that car accident that happened years before. It was the result of having a dysregulated nervous system. Practicing Kundalini yoga has eased that chronic pain and I have not experienced a migraine since I began practicing. It's been over two years now. The chronic pain is gone and so are all the muscle relaxers and pain medication that I used to take.

The unique combination of repetitive movements followed by periods of stillness in Kundalini yoga serves as a process for re-educating the nervous system. Practicing Kundalini yoga can help reestablish stability and resilience in the nervous system. It also promotes balance of glandular secretions in the body and not just the ones related to stress responses, but also the ones that support relaxation, connection, digestion and sleep cycles.

Being unable to relax is common for people with PTSD and when you are unable to relax, the balance of the nervous system gets off track. Rebalancing it through yoga revitalizes our life force, oxygenates our blood, refreshes and purifies the organs and enables muscles and tissue to renew quicker. This also helps rebalance the mind, stabilize emotions, as well as renew and upgrade our entire being so we can begin to thrive. Can you see now how this practice can help a nervous system that has been dysregulated by a post traumatic injury?

A typical Kundalini practice is focused on control of breath, expansion of energy and aligning the chakras. The practice begins with the opening chanting, which is also known as "tuning in", followed by a brief warm up for your spine. After the warm up, the kriya begins. Kriya is a sequence of postures that involve movement, breathing techniques, mindfulness and mantra. Once the kriya is complete, there is a relaxation period, known as Savasana, followed by meditation. The meditation can include mantras (chanting), mudras (hand positions) and breathing techniques known as pranayama. The practice concludes with the closing mantra or a song.

You don't need to believe in chakras or be spiritual to enjoy the benefits of Kundalini yoga. You just need to have an open mind about trying new things.

If you really can't imagine yourself doing yoga, there are a couple of other options. Tai chi and Qi Gong are other types of traditional practices. The gentle movement of these practices have all been shown as effective ways to calm the nervous system as well.

Chapter 15

Relaxing the Nervous System

In addition to yoga, there are a few other ways to help regulate the nervous system. The following activities are things I practice and have played a huge part in helping to regulate my nervous system. For me, it wasn't a matter of choosing between yoga and the following activities. I do all of these activities in order to keep my nervous system regulated.

Breathing Exercises

Deep breathing exercises help to oxygenate the blood and are one of the quickest ways to calm the nervous system. There are several types of deep breathing exercises that can help but the easiest one is to inhale very deeply through the nose while expanding your abdomen and chest. Hold the air inside for a moment before exhaling all the air completely out through the mouth. While you're doing this, try to focus only on the flow of air entering your nose, lungs and belly.

There is another breathing exercise that I like as well. This is probably the simplest method to come down from a state of high anxiety quickly. It's my go to method and I use it a lot. It's called box breathing and goes like this:

- breathe in for a count of four

- hold the breath in for a count of four

- release the breath for a count of four

- keep your lungs empty for a count of four

-repeat the process as long as necessary

After just a couple of rounds of breathing this way I usually feel calmer. I use this method a lot and it also helps to stop a full blown panic attack from happening. I also use this method to help slow down anxious thoughts when they arise, and I also use it during meditation sometimes. This is a great breathing exercise to use for reducing any kind of stress or anxiety that comes up.

Movement

This isn't to say you need to start jogging, unless that's your thing. Even moderate movement can have a positive impact on the nervous system. Walking, jogging and dancing are all great options for helping to relieve stress and create awareness in your body. For me it's walking and hiking. I try to walk a minimum of 5 kilometres everyday. My preference is hiking in nature though, and I do it every chance I get. It's calm and quiet in nature. I find it very therapeutic and beneficial in helping to clear away unwanted thoughts. I've also been known to turn up the music and dance around in my kitchen from time to time.

Chanting and Singing

Chanting and singing are both excellent ways to help the nervous system relax. Chanting and singing allow your breathing to slow down. It also stimulates the vagus nerve, which can become overactive after traumatic experiences. An overactive vagus nerve can lead to anxiety, changes in mood, pain and nausea.

Chanting and singing can also be an effective way for expressing emotions. Do you ever notice how good it feels when you sing your favorite song as loud as you can? It feels good because it's good for your nervous system. You've got nothing to lose, so turn up the music and start singing.

Meditation

I realize that it's quite difficult for some people to sit with their thoughts in meditation. Especially when PTSD is involved. For some people, meditation is difficult because it may feel like you are letting your guard down by entering this state of relaxation. Or it may become a time when the negative, intrusive thoughts creep in. It was a bit difficult for me in the beginning of this journey as well, even though I already had a somewhat regular meditation practice. If meditation is challenging for you due to unwanted thoughts, please understand that it will eventually get better.

I'm a huge believer in meditation and I feel that is an extremely beneficial practice, which is why I obtained a certification to be able to teach it. You may not like the thoughts that come up during meditation, but that's one of the purposes of it. To observe your thoughts and emotions. How can you expect to deal with your thoughts and emotions if you avoid letting them come to the surface?

Research has shown that a meditation practice can strengthen neural connections and even change the structure of the brain. You don't have to meditate for long periods of time if it's challenging for you. Sitting in meditation for as little as five minutes a day can be beneficial.

There are different types of meditations you can do. If you're brand new to meditating, I suggest trying a short guided meditation. A guided meditation helps if you're trying to avoid difficult thoughts in the beginning. Rather than observing your thoughts, you're listening and going where the guide takes you. Typically, the guide will instruct you on how to relax your body and then lead you through visualizations and mental images. You can find a variety of free guided meditations of any length on YouTube.

My main meditation technique stems from Zen meditation and is a type of quiet awareness. During this type of meditation, the main goal is learning how to allow your thoughts to flow freely through the mind, without judging or rejecting them. There is no real goal of this meditation other than to just sit and allow your mind to just be. Let the thoughts come, observe the thoughts, don't judge them and let the thoughts pass by.

Practicing meditation has taught me to notice my thoughts even when I'm not meditating. And they are definitely not as dark and catastrophic as they once were. I enjoy and look forward to meditating. I get some of my best ideas and insights during meditation. In fact, the idea for this book came to me while I was in meditation.

Have you noticed that meditation, breathing exercises, movement and chanting have been mentioned here and all of them are also part of Kundalini yoga? There is a reason why this yoga is so effective at helping to regulate the nervous system.

Cold Plunges

I first learned about cold plunging by following Wim Hof. If you're not familiar with Wim Hof, he is a Dutch extreme athlete and motivational speaker who is known as "The Iceman". He is quite a remarkable individual who held a Guinness World Record for swimming under ice. He holds a record for running a half marathon barefoot on ice and snow and he climbed to an altitude of 7400 metres on Mount Everest wearing only shorts and runners.

He invented what is called the Wim Hof Method and it includes breathing exercises in addition to the cold plunging. I've tried his breathing method a few times, however I found it to be almost anxiety inducing so I don't practice it.

I have done the cold water though. Not a plunge, but turning the shower to just cold water for a minute or two. It was difficult in the beginning but I kind of got used to it. I find it to be a shock to the system but I feel great afterwards.

Cold therapy has been proven to help regulate the nervous system and improve anxiety and depression. I'm not a person who enjoys the cold at all, however I was willing to try it if it could help improve the regulation of my nervous system. It's amazing what we are willing to try when we are feeling desperate for relief.

If you're interested in learning more about the Wim Hof Method, I suggest following him on YouTube where he demonstrates and will guide you through his breathing technique. Just keep in mind that the type of breathing he teaches isn't effective for everyone with a post traumatic injury so it's best to do a little research before giving it a try.

Chapter 16

Journaling, Mindfulness and Connection

In addition to the activities that help regulate the nervous system, there are other activities that have helped me achieve a healthy mind/body balance. The following activities have also helped to get me to where I am today.

Journaling

I'm sure you've had people suggesting you journal your feelings. I know I did. In the beginning of my journey, I did not enjoy journaling so much. I tried it and I did not enjoy writing about my feelings and emotions. Of course I didn't. Not only was I in denial, but I was so emotionally dysregulated that I was numb most of the time and didn't always know how I was feeling. Also, for me, writing my feelings down also meant they were real. And then I would have to acknowledge them. If they stayed in my head, I could keep convincing myself things were not so bad. That maybe I'm exaggerating or blowing things out of proportion. That's what being in denial looks like.

In the beginning of this journey I started by just writing about the nightmares I was having. It felt safe enough because dreams aren't real so I wasn't actually writing about my feelings. The only feeling I had from these nightmares was paralyzing fear.

A lot of my nightmares directly involved certain clients I'd had when I was a CCW. So writing about my nightmares morphed into writing about these clients. Rather than the typical way people journal, I wrote like I was telling a story. I wrote as though others would be reading it. Not only did I write about the clients, I was eventually able to write my own experiences and feelings in a similar way. Reading these stories afterwards was like reading a story that happened to someone else. Whenever traumatic events happened to other people, I was always able to have compassion for those people, so why couldn't I have any compassion for myself? I was always beating myself up for feeling fear or having any negative emotions. By learning to write this way, I was able to view my experiences in a different way. I learned to have compassion for myself.

Journaling can also be a good way to release stressful emotions you may be feeling. For some people just writing everything down can help reduce some stress. I've known people who just purge all their negative feelings by writing them down and then never actually reading it again. If you're going to try journaling, you need to find a way that works for you. There is no right or wrong way to journal. It's a personal practice so do whatever feels right for you.

Journaling can create a new awareness about some of the situations you've been in. Sometimes just writing things down and reading them later can help you form new perceptions about those situations. That's exactly what happened when I switched the way I was journaling. It gave me the gift of self compassion, which changed so much in my life.

Learning to journal the way I did changed everything for me. I had been writing for a while and one day while I was in meditation, the idea came to me to share what I had been writing about. So I decided to start a blog. I was terrified the first time I shared what I'd written. But I also felt lighter and more free than I had felt in a very long time. It was a very therapeutic experience.

After writing a few blog posts, I felt called to write this book. So you never know where journaling might lead you. Maybe you have a book waiting to come out of you as well. No matter what your goal might be, journaling can be a wonderful way to become more self aware and learn self compassion.

A Mindfulness Practice

A mindfulness practice will help you to be focused and aware of the present moment. Simply put, it keeps you focused and engaged in the present moment, the here and now and not distracted by intrusive thoughts of the past or worry about the future.

Spending time in nature and photography are my mindfulness practices. Getting out in nature to take photos helps me stay grounded and observing everything around me helps keep me in the present moment. I've learned it's almost impossible to be anxious and panicked while being immersed in the safety and beauty of nature looking for photo opportunities. This is also true when I'm editing my photos.

There are so many activities that promote mindfulness by helping to keep you in the present moment. Getting active or creative is something everyone can do. You just have to find something that you're passionate about, something that lights you up, and go for it.

Connection

Finding people who are supportive and can relate to what you've experienced is important. Friends and family can be a great means of support, but it is also important to connect with others who are walking similar paths. This type of connection has played a vital part in my recovery.

In the very beginning of my journey I connected with a past coworker who had also been on a similar path. This was tremendously helpful in making me feel less alone. A few months later I began attending peer support meetings with people who understood my struggles. Yes, it was scary in the beginning. Walking into a group of strangers felt very intimidating at first, but I soon realized that I had nothing to fear. These people were all there to support each other. Finding a place where I felt safe to share and engage with others who understood helped me feel less alone. I will be forever grateful for the compassion and support I received while attending these meetings.

Chapter 17

Making the Decision to Try Microdosing Psilocybin

A year ago I thought my recovery was as good as it was ever going to get. And it wasn't where I had hoped to be. I had heard about people microdosing psilocybin mushrooms. I didn't know much about it at the time, but I became intrigued immediately. The day of that appointment with Dr. Pill Pusher, I decided to do some research because if it could be helpful, then I figured I had nothing to lose by trying it.

The medications that are typically prescribed for PTSD can alleviate some of the symptoms, but they do not replace the work required for recovery to take place. These medications do not cure PTSD. In my opinion, they are like putting a bandaid on a wound. It helps to protect that wound but does nothing to actually heal it.

As I've mentioned, I am definitely not anti medication. I just didn't feel like medication was the right choice in my recovery for a few reasons and to be honest, I was more afraid of taking pills from the pharmacy than I was of trying the magic mushrooms. If you're using pharmaceutical medication for your recovery, that's okay. Everyone is different and needs to find what works for them. There is absolutely no judgment here. I'm simply sharing my reasons for taking the route I took.

I don't believe these types of medications are something that should be taken forever either, and stopping them can be difficult. I have known people who struggled hard when coming off of antidepressants, which is one of the biggest reasons I did not want to take it. I also had no interest in taking medication that was manufactured in a lab when there are plants growing in our world that can achieve better results, without the unwanted side effects. I did not want the emotional numbing that comes with these types of medications. I had been emotionally numb from the PTSD for so long and honestly, I just wanted to have feelings again.

First, I need to say that it is illegal to possess psilocybin mushrooms and I do not promote illegal activity. However, I have made the personal choice to use psilocybin as part of my recovery plan. Canada is beginning to recognize that psilocybin can be beneficial in the treatment of PTSD and other conditions. On January 5, 2022, Health Canada made amendments to the Special Access Program, allowing medical practitioners to request access to some psychedelics for eligible patients. I've recently been informed that

I am eligible for using psychedelics to treat my PTSD, so now it's a waiting game. We all know how slow these processes can be, so in the meantime I will continue to use it on my own because it has made an incredible difference in my life.

Chapter 18

The Protocols

Before making the decision to microdose, I watched some documentaries and I began following the work of James Fadiman, whose work can be explored by checking out his website. I also followed the work of Paul Stamets, whose work can be found here: .

Dr. James Fadiman is known as "The Father of Microdosing" and is a prominent figure in the field of psychedelic research. Although psychedelic research was banned in the 1970's, Dr. Fadiman continued exploring and became an advocate for microdosing and developed his own protocol. He believes that microdosing can help people gain balance in their lives and enhance connections with their bodies. After microdosing psilocybin, I completely agree with this.

In 2011, Dr. James Fadiman published his book, The Psychedelic Explorer's Guide: Safe, Therapeutic, and Sacred Journeys. His book explores microdosing as a kind of subculture in the world of psychedelic use. Many indigenous cultures have used microdosing for years. Dr. Fadiman's book formally introduced the term "microdosing" into the mainstream and awakened people's curiosity about the benefits microdosing could offer them.

A microdosing protocol is like a structured schedule for how much, how often and for how long to take a psychedelic drug. I tried two different protocols in order to find the one that works best for me.

The Fadiman protocol is a safe and controlled way to use psychedelic medicine and is a great place to start if you're a beginner. The small amount taken is meant to feel slight changes without the hallucinogenic effects. The Fadiman protocol is taking a micro dose one day and then two days with no dose. It is recommended to do this for four weeks with a two week break in between so a tolerance isn't built up. This also allows the mind and body to return to a baseline state. It also allows time for reflection, integration of experiences and maintaining a balanced approach to microdosing. The day you take a micro dose, it is advised that you write the effects it had on you in a journal. Keeping track of your feelings will help you determine if you need to adjust the dose.

***

Paul Stamets is a renowned mycologist and advocate of medicinal and psychedelic fungi. He has made significant contributions to fields such as bee conservation, environmental cleanup, and sustainable building materials. He is the author of six books and has explored the use of psychedelic medicine, in particular, the therapeutic benefits of psilocybin mushrooms. I have much respect and gratitude for this man's research and his contributions to the betterment of the world.

Paul Stamets developed the Stamets Stack protocol for microdosing psilocybin mushrooms. This protocol involves combining psilocybin mushrooms, Lion's mane mushrooms, and niacin (vitamin B3) to enhance cognition and promote neuroregeneration.

Lion's mane mushrooms are non-psychedelic and have been used in traditional Chinese medicine. Research suggests they may improve cognitive impairment and they may also reduce symptoms of depression and anxiety.

Niacin is also known as vitamin B3. This vitamin plays an important role in energy production and also supports the health of skin and the nervous system. The purpose of Niacin in the Stamets Stack is to act as a flushing agent, helping the delivery of the beneficial compounds to the brain.

Psilocybin is found in magic mushrooms. Psilocybin is a classic psychedelic that can alter perception, mood, and cognition. Research has suggested it may reduce depression and anxiety and stimulate neurogenesis. This can potentially enhance intelligence, kindness, and courage.

The dosage for the stack can vary but the recommendation is as follows; for psilocybin mushrooms, the recommended dosage is 0.1 to 1 gram of Psilocybe cubensis, which constitutes a microdose. Lion's mane mushrooms should be consumed in a range of 5 to 20 grams. As for Niacin (Vitamin B3), the recommended dosage is 100 to 200 milligrams. I've adjusted the psilocybin a couple of times to achieve my desired results. I follow the dose recommendation on the Lion's mane that I purchase, as it is liquid drops rather than whole mushrooms. And the Niacin I use is 100mg. It is important to use the Niacin that causes a flush. The non-flushing type is not recommended for use in this stack.

The Stamets protocol involves taking this stack four days in a row and then taking a three day break. During the break you may continue taking the Lion's mane. This cycle is repeated for four weeks. Once the four weeks are completed, a break for two to four weeks is recommended before resuming the protocol.

The Stamets Stack is believed to have several benefits for cognitive function and neurological growth. There are eleven potential benefits of the Stamets Stack, as explained by Paul Stamets. These benefits include the following:

1. The stack promotes neurogenesis, meaning it may support the growth of new neurons in the brain.

2. Reduces anxiety and depression. People using this stack

may experience a decrease in the feelings of anxiety and depression.

3. The stack has the potential to enhance memory and cognitive abilities.

4. Improvements in motor skill and coordination.

5. The stack may help with achieving a more stable and balanced mood.

6. Users of this stack may experience an increase in creative thinking and problem-solving abilities.

7. Improved hearing and vision means the stack may contribute to individuals experiencing better auditory and visual perception.

8. Greater sense of interconnection. Users of the stack may feel a stronger sense of connection with others and the world around them.

9. Relief from PTSD symptoms. The stack may provide relief from symptoms associated with Post Traumatic Stress Disorder.

10. Increased ability to socialize, empathize, and feel courageous, meaning people who use this stack may experience improvements in social interactions, empathy, and courage.

11. The stack may help to promote a deeper sense of self-awareness.

Overall, the Stamets Stack was designed to enhance brain function and encourage novel and adaptive thinking. It has also been suggested that these effects can potentially contribute to the evolution of human consciousness.

The most important thing to consider before trying this protocol or any other protocol, is the fact that psilocybin mushrooms are illegal to possess in many countries. Other important considerations for the Stamets Stack are to do with Niacin.

Niacin can make allergies worse by increasing histamine. It can also interact with alcohol and certain medications so it's good to talk to a health care provider before taking it. Also, Niacin is not recommended for individuals with liver disease, kidney disease, diabetes, gout, or peptic ulcer disease, so please talk to your healthcare provider before taking it if any of these conditions apply to you.

Niacin also causes flushing effects which may include temporary skin redness, tingling, and itching. This happens to me, but mainly when I take it on an empty stomach, however, the effects are very short lived and I don't find it too uncomfortable.

The use of psychedelics is not recommended if you suffer from psychosis, schizophrenia, or severe anxiety. Overdoing a microdose could lead to manic states, potentially making the underlying condition worse. Again, if any of these conditions apply to you, please consult your healthcare provider before taking psilocybin.

Chapter 19

Preparing to Microdose

It is recommended that before you begin any microdosing protocol, that you journal your moods and feelings in general daily for at least a couple of weeks. Journaling your moods & feelings for a couple of weeks is important. This way you can monitor and see patterns in your moods and once you begin micro dosing, you will be able to see any differences and know for sure if it's helping.

It is also recommended to start your first dose on a good day and not one where you're too stressed out or feeling other negative emotions. The reason for this is that psilocybin tends to amplify how you're feeling. So taking it when you're having a bad day or feeling off might increase those bad feelings and deter you from continuing.

After researching the different types of psilocybin mushrooms, I chose to go with Golden Teachers. From everything I've read, they are one of the milder types and are recommended for beginners.

I was able to obtain 100mg capsules which is the recommended starting dose.

I take my microdose in the morning. It is advised to take it before 10am to mitigate the effects it may have on sleep. Microdosing has never interfered with my sleep, but perhaps it's because I've always taken it in the morning. It is also advised to take it in the morning because the purpose of it is to enhance your daily life.

It's important to follow your regular daily routine while microdosing. Except the day you take your very first dose. The first time I took a microdose I made sure it was a day I would be staying at home. This is recommended in case there are any adverse effects. I had none.

There is a lot of information out there about growing your own mushrooms, drying them out and crushing them up to put into capsules for microdosing. I found it was easier to obtain them already measured into capsules. Growing my own is something I am interested in doing, however, I'm not sure how to measure the amount of psilocybin in each mushroom. So it just seems easier to purchase them from a Mycologist who knows what they're doing.

I'm now able to get my psilocybin in a concentrated liquid formula. A couple of drops on a piece of pineapple and I'm done. No taste and the liquid is faster acting.

Chapter 20

My Experience Microdosing Psilocybin

I began microdosing by using James Fadiman's protocol. I did this for approximately three months and I did notice some benefits. I felt a bit more energy and motivation as well as an improvement in my overall mood. I also started seeing some of my PTSD symptoms with curiosity rather than the usual dread. Dissociation can be scary when it happens, but psilocybin has taken the fear out of it and replaced that fear with curiosity. Being able to view my symptoms in this way has made some of them a bit easier to live with.

After getting comfortable with this protocol, I switched to Paul Stamets protocol. This is when the real changes began happening for me.

After the first month of using Paul Stamets protocol, I noticed some incredible improvements and benefits. And after a few months, I feel like a newer and improved version of myself. I have worked hard on bettering myself through this journey so not all the credit goes to psilocybin. But with that said, psilocybin has definitely improved my quality of life and opened my mind to so many possibilities.

Some of the benefits I get from microdosing psilocybin are:

1. It's been easier for me to stay in the present moment. This is really helpful, especially when it comes to anxiety. Rather than my anxious thoughts taking over and getting the best of me, I am better able to guide my mind back to the moment in front of me. The only moment that really matters.

2. It's given me a different perspective on some of my symptoms. I am no longer afraid when I experience dissociation or panic attacks because I am able to view them with curiosity. And because I can view these moments in this way, I am able to understand why it's happening, which makes them easier to get through.

3. I feel like it slows my reaction time to panic attacks. It's hard to describe, but it's almost like I'm seeing things happen in slow motion or like time is paused for a few seconds. This brief pause in time gives me the chance to

recognize what is happening and allows me a second to start breathing my way through it with more ease than I've ever experienced. It doesn't always stop a panic attack from happening but it's definitely easier to manage when it feels like I'm seeing all the stages in slow motion. Since my panic does not elevate as quickly, it makes it easier to talk myself down and I don't feel like I'm about to die.

4. It's helping me with my trigger responses. Because of the feeling of slow motion or time being paused for a few seconds, I've been able to notice that I'm triggered almost right away. And because of that awareness, I'm able to stay more calm than I've ever been able to when I'm triggered. In that brief moment where time seems paused, I'm able to tell myself I'm okay, I'm just triggered right now but I'm safe. Because of this, I'm able to have a more rational reaction to the triggering event. I still feel panicky in these situations but not in the same out of control way I used to.

5. There are times when I still feel like I've fallen down into that dark hole. Since I started microdosing psilocybin, I understand what happened to send me down there and it feels a bit easier to pull myself out of it. It's not a miracle cure, but all of these small improvements help to give me a better quality of life.

6. I am still hyper vigilant and I'm pretty sure I always

will be. But my startle response has relaxed significantly. Everything used to make me jump. I'm still jumpy at times but nothing like I used to be.

7. In general, I feel lighter and more energetic most days. Like the weight of the world has been lifted away from me.

8. I feel more inspired, it's easier to focus and my creativity has increased. I especially notice this when I sit down to write.

9. I can see clearly how everything is connected. People, animals, plants, nature, the stars, the sun, the moon and the earth. We are all part of the universe and we are all connected.

10. I have more insight and self awareness. I can see more clearly than ever how everything and everyone from my past has made me who I am today. I can view things that happened in the past without regret. Instead I see that everything that's happened in my life were lessons. Lessons leading me to live my true purpose. Like I said, everything is connected.

11. Because I have more insight, I've been able to discuss difficult things I've experienced with more ease. This helped a few times in therapy.

12. I feel more peace, love and joy in my heart. This has helped me feel lighter, happier and more peaceful than I've ever felt before.

There is no pill created in a lab that can do this for me. But psilocybin does and it does so without unwanted side effects, no dependency and no withdrawal. Although I'm sure Dr. Pill Pusher would disagree with me on this.

Microdosing psilocybin has taken my trauma recovery to the next level. I would not be where I am today without these mushrooms. They are amazing medicine, a true gift from nature. I have not experienced any adverse side effects. They are not addictive, although you can build up a tolerance to them, and that is why microdosing protocols require you to take a break every few weeks.

I have been microdosing psilocybin for a year. It's taken a bit of trial and error making adjustments to find the right dose but I finally found the right amount for me. Using psilocybin has helped take my recovery from the plateau I was experiencing to the next level and I am so grateful for that.

You may be wondering if the effects of psilocybin stop during the times you are on a tolerance break. In my experience, that happened a bit when I first started microdosing. Once I began Paul Stamets protocol and found the right dosage for me, it happened much less. On a two week break I still feel the benefits but into week three they begin to dissipate and some of my PTSD symptoms intensify a bit. Once I restart the protocol, the negative symptoms become much more manageable again.

You may also be wondering how you will know if you're taking the right dose for you. I started at the lowest recommended dose mainly because I was afraid of what might happen if I took too much. The capsules I started with were 100mg which is approximately one tenth of a gram. I thought this was the perfect amount at the beginning. Once I got the concentrated drops I was taking two drops which is equivalent to 120mg. This dose was working better for me.

I put my microdose drops on a piece of pineapple to make it easy to take. One day, three drops accidentally came out onto the pineapple rather than two. I looked at it for a minute and wondered if I should eat it. I decided to go for it because I knew an extra drop wouldn't cause hallucinations. This is how I accidentally discovered the perfect dose for me.

Increasing your dose is a good idea if there's little or no change in your state of mind. But it's always better to start low and increase it until you achieve the desired effects. With that being said, even once you find the perfect dose for you, it may need to be increased after a while if your tolerance has been built up. You'll know when it's time to increase your dosage by how you're feeling and also by monitoring your feelings and moods in a journal. That's why journaling is an important part of this process.

Now that I am familiar with and comfortable taking psilocybin, I will take it on the days that are not so good. In the beginning I wouldn't have but now I find it helps even when my mood is low. I wouldn't recommend doing this in the beginning though. If your mood is negative, it may enhance those negative feelings and you may not want to try taking another dose. My advice would be to get familiar with psilocybin and how it affects you before experimenting further.

Chapter 21

Final Thoughts on Microdosing

There is a lot more research done on the benefits of taking larger doses of psilocybin to treat anxiety, depression and addiction. I am open to this experience, however I am waiting for it to be an approved therapy in Canada. Taking a large dose on my own is not something I'm ready to try. I would like my experience to be in a therapeutic environment where I am able to integrate the experience with a therapist.

There has been very little research done on the effects of microdosing, however psilocybin has a long history of safe use. Research suggests using it in such small doses appears to be safe. And from my experience of using it, it's been safe for me and has given me some amazing results.

I plan to continue microdosing psilocybin because it has been very beneficial to my recovery. The pros definitely outweigh the cons and the benefits have been amazing. And if I decide one day that I don't want to take it anymore, there will be no withdrawal symptoms to worry about.

I'm not suggesting that you should run out and try it or that it will be the magic cure you're looking for. It's definitely not for everyone. I'm just sharing my experience with you to provide some insight on microdosing. If you're interested in trying to microdose psychedelics, my advice to you is to do some of your own research and proceed with caution. And please remember, if you have any medical conditions or are taking any medications, speak to your healthcare provider before starting.

I started by watching the following documentaries before I began following the work of James Fadiman and Paul Stamets:

How to Change Your Mind

Fantastic Fungi

From Shock to Awe

Additionally, I read about a few different people's personal experiences microdosing different types of psychedelics. I also followed the microdosing journey of a complex trauma survivor on YouTube.

My hope is that one day psilocybin mushrooms are no longer illegal. It is medicine that can help many people who are suffering. Like I said, I do not promote illegal activity, however when it benefits my mental health in such profound ways, I'll take the risk.

Chapter 22

Conclusion

All these changes I've made in my life are now part of my new way of living. Yoga, meditation, psilocybin and writing are not just part of my recovery anymore. They are some of the things I need to do in order to maintain the level of recovery I've achieved.

Stopping yoga and meditation is not an option for me. There have been times when I have been away on vacation and not had the opportunity to do yoga every day. After I miss a couple of days, things can really start going sideways. The pain slowly starts creeping back into my neck and shoulders and my mind, body and soul feel completely out of alignment. If I let my practice go, I'm afraid it wouldn't be long before I had a migraine again.

This is why I say trauma recovery is about learning a new way to live. A way that keeps your mind and body healthy and your nervous system regulated. Recovery is a lifestyle. And like any lifestyle, there are requirements for maintaining that lifestyle.

Sometimes I wonder if I would have been further ahead in my recovery sooner if I had discovered psilocybin earlier. But I will never know the answer to that. And that's one of the benefits of using psilocybin, I no longer spend much time wondering about and regretting the past. I'm currently only concerned with the present moment, but I am optimistic about my future.

About the Author

Darcy has held different positions in the Department of Justice where she worked in both Institutional and Community Corrections. After a post traumatic injury derailed her career and life, she embarked on a journey of healing, self discovery and transformation.

This journey led her to pursue an education in alternative healing, where she earned a Master of Alternative Therapies & Natural Medicine Diploma. In addition, her interest in using psychedelics for post traumatic recovery inspired her to learn more. Through the Psychedelic Support Network, she received a certificate for Understanding Psilocybin: Effects, Neurobiology, and Therapeutic Approaches, and Microdosing Psilocybin & LSD: What We Know So Far. She is passionate about continuing to learn as much as possible about post traumatic injuries, recovery and helping to inspire others through their own recovery journeys.

Made in United States
Troutdale, OR
11/21/2023